CONTENTS

GRADE 4

UNIT 1 SENTENCES

GRAMMAR SENTENCES

Sentences 1

Declarative and Interrogative Sentences 2

Imperative and Exclamatory Sentences 3

Combining Sentences: Compound Sentences 4

Mechanics and Usage: Sentence Punctuation 5

Mixed Review 6

Complete Subjects and Complete Predicates 7

Simple Subjects 8

Simple Predicates 9

Combining Sentences: Compound Subjects 10

Combining Sentences: Compound Predicates 11

Mechanics and Usage: Correcting Run-on Sentences 12

Mixed Review 13

Common Errors with Sentence Fragments and Run-on Sentences 14

BUILD SKILLS

Study Skills: Note-Taking and Summarizing 15

Vocabulary: Time-Order Words 16

Composition: Main Idea 17

UNIT 2 NOUNS

GRAMMAR NOUNS

Nouns 18

Singular and Plural Nouns 19

Nouns Ending with *y* 20

More Plural Nouns 21

Common and Proper Nouns 22

Mechanics and Usage: Capitalization 23

Mixed Review 24

Singular Possessive Nouns 25

Plural Possessive Nouns 26

Combining Sentences: Nouns 27

Mechanics and Usage: Abbreviations 28

Mixed Review 29

Common Errors with Plurals and Possessives 30

BUILD SKILLS

Study Skills: Parts of a Book 31

Vocabulary: Compound Words 32

Composition: Writing Descriptions 33

UNIT 3 VERBS

GRAMMAR VERBS

Action Verbs	34
Verb Tenses	35
Subject-Verb Agreement	36
Spelling Present-Tense and Past-Tense Verbs	37
Mechanics and Usage: Commas in a Series	38
Mixed Review	39
Main Verbs and Helping Verbs	40
Using Helping Verbs	41
Linking Verbs	42
Using Linking Verbs	43
Irregular Verbs	44
More Irregular Verbs	45
Mechanics and Usage: Contractions with *Not*	46
Mixed Review	47
Common Errors in Subject-Verb Agreement	48

BUILD SKILLS

Study Skills: Card Catalog	49
Vocabulary: Prefixes	50
Composition: Leads and Endings	51

UNIT 4 ADJECTIVES

GRAMMAR ADJECTIVES

Adjectives	52
Articles: *a, an, the*	53
Adjectives After Linking Verbs	54
Mechanics and Usage: Proper Adjectives	55
Mixed Review	56
Adjectives That Compare	57
Spelling Adjectives That Compare	58
Comparing with *More* and *Most*	59
Comparing with *Good* and *Bad*	60
Combining Sentences: Adjectives	61
Mechanics and Usage: Letter Punctuation	62
Mixed Review	63
Common Errors with Adjectives	64

BUILD SKILLS

Study Skills: Maps	65
Vocabulary: Synonyms and Antonyms	66
Composition: Organization	67

UNIT 5 PRONOUNS

GRAMMAR PRONOUNS

Pronouns 68
Subject Pronouns 69
Object Pronouns 70
Mechanics and Usage: Punctuation in Dialogue 71
Mixed Review 72
Pronoun-Verb Agreement 73
Combining Sentences: Subject and Object Pronouns 74
Possessive Pronouns 75
Mechanics and Usage: Contractions—Pronouns and Verbs 76
Mixed Review 77
Common Errors with Pronouns 78

BUILD SKILLS

Study Skills: Dictionary 79
Vocabulary: Homophones and Homographs 80
Composition: Writing Dialogue 81

UNIT 6 Adverbs and Prepositions

GRAMMAR Adverbs and Prepositions

Adverbs That Tell *How* 82

Adverbs That Tell *When* or *Where* 83

Adverbs That Compare 84

More Adverbs That Compare 85

Mechanics and Usage: *Good* and *Well* 86

Mixed Review 87

Negatives 88

Prepositions 89

Prepositional Phrases 90

Combining Sentences: Complex Sentences 91

Mechanics and Usage: Commas 92

Mixed Review 93

Common Errors with Adverbs 94

BUILD SKILLS

Study Skills: Encyclopedia 95

Vocabulary: Suffixes 96

Composition: Outlining 97

ANSWERS T1–T49

Name________________________________ Date______________ **Extend 1**

Sentences

Read the posters. Change each fragment to a complete sentence. Then use complete sentences to rewrite the posters in the blank boxes.

Bright Teeth

Perfect Smile

You need: Glow-White Toothpaste.

Free toothbrush with first purchase

Enter the Art Contest.

Everyone Welcome!

Entry forms must be in by April 8, 2006.

All drawings, paintings, collages accepted.

Prizes!

At Home: Why are sentence fragments effective in posters and some kinds of advertisements? Explain.

▶ **Critical Thinking**

Name ____________________ Date __________ **Extend 2**

Declarative and Interrogative Sentences

The following sentences are either questions or answers for a trivia game. Next to each, write **D** if it is a declarative sentence or **I** if it is an interrogative sentence. Rewrite each sentence and punctuate it correctly. Then draw lines to match each question and answer.

I	II
1. it is Montpelier ______	**a.** it is known for dairy products ______
____________________	____________________
2. Florida is a peninsula ______	**b.** what is the capital of Vermont ______
____________________	____________________
3. where do penguins live ______	**c.** what is the 50th state ______
____________________	____________________
4. it's a group of islands called Hawaii ______	**d.** what kind of landform is Florida ______
____________________	____________________
5. what is Wisconsin known for ______	**e.** it was Betsy Ross ______
____________________	____________________
6. who designed the first U.S. flag ______	**f.** they live in Antarctica ______
____________________	____________________

At Home: Add five more interrogative and declarative sentences to this game.

▶ **Critical Thinking**

Name______________________________ Date____________ **Extend 3**

Imperative and Exclamatory Sentences

Three types of sentences are included below. Draw one line under each imperative sentence. Draw two lines under each exclamatory sentence. Then write the sentences in paragraph form. Remember to use correct punctuation.

1. I can hardly believe it
2. I am learning to play tennis
3. Just watch me hit the ball
4. Oh, how hard my teacher makes me work
5. She makes me jog around the court to keep fit
6. No way can I jog around it 5 times
7. Then we volley back and forth
8. Wait until you see how much I have improved
9. Hit a ball to me and you will see
10. Tennis is a terrific game

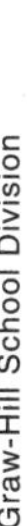

At Home: What do you know how to do? Write a paragraph titled "How to make a pizza" or "How I learned to play..." Include both exclamatory and imperative sentences.

▶ **Critical Thinking**

Name ______________________ Date ____________ **Extend 4**

Combining Sentences: Compound Sentences

A. Combine the following pairs of sentences using *and, or,* or *but.* Write each new sentence on the lines.

1. Listen to my riddle. ______________________

Tell me the answer. ______________________

____

2. This coat has no sleeves. ______________________

It has no buttons. ______________________

____

3. It has no pockets. ______________________

It won't keep you warm. ______________________

____

4. Do you know the answer? ______________________

Can you make a guess? ______________________

____

5. I bet you know. ______________________

I'll tell you anyway. ______________________

____

B. Write your answer to the riddle.

____

At Home: Combine the following sentences to include in a cartoon strip. "It is dark inside. I will not go in." Write the sentence in a speech bubble. Add three more frames to the strip.

▶ **Critical Thinking**

Name____________________ Date__________ **Extend 5**

Mechanics and Usage: Sentence Punctuation

Read the letter. Ask yourself if each sentence is declarative, interrogative, imperative, or exclamatory. Then rewrite the paragraph on the lines below. Add the correct punctuation.

Dear Rosa,

what a great Saturday I had listen to this

my parents took me on a nature hike on the trail we saw a chipmunk and we saw some weird-looking birds' nests I wanted to get a close look at a turtle in the brook you won't believe this I fell into the brook and I got my shoes and clothes all wet that water was so cold I began to shiver mom and dad gave me their sweaters Just then, a long green snake slithered from under the log have you ever seen one I was scared and I ran right into the arms of my dad we all had a good laugh I can't wait to go on a nature hike again Come with us next time.

Your pen pal,
Yolanda

At Home: Pretend you are Rosa. Write a letter to Yolanda. What would you tell her? Use different types of sentences. Punctuate your letter correctly.

▶ **Critical Thinking**

Mixed Review

A. Write an interrogative sentence about each topic listed. Use the correct punctuation.

1. breakfast: ____________________

2. transportation to school: ____________________

3. today's lunch: ____________________

4. after-school sports: ____________________

5. homework: ____________________

B. Write a declarative sentence about each topic. Punctuate correctly. Make sure that at least two of your sentences are compound.

6. airport: ____________________

7. luggage: ____________________

8. ticket: ____________________

9. flight attendant: ____________________

10. destination: ____________________

C. Write an imperative or an exclamatory sentence about each topic.

11. lost in a department store: ____________________

12. security guard: ____________________

13. new shoes: ____________________

14. not enough money: ____________________

15. new way home: ____________________

At Home: Write five compound sentences using *and, but,* or *or* to combine them. Share your work with a family member.

▶ **Critical Thinking**

Name______________________________ Date____________ **Extend 7**

Complete Subjects and Complete Predicates

Draw one line under the complete subject. Draw two lines under the complete predicate of each sentence.

My uncle Joe loves to fish. He wakes up before the sun rises and climbs into his small rowboat. Uncle Joe rows down the river. He returns home about midday with a bucket of medium-sized fish. (My Aunt Rita will cook them later for dinner.) Uncle Joe takes off for the country store.

My uncle tells his pals at the store that he had a huge fish on his line. He says that the fish got away because a little boy distracted him.

His story is a very fishy tale.

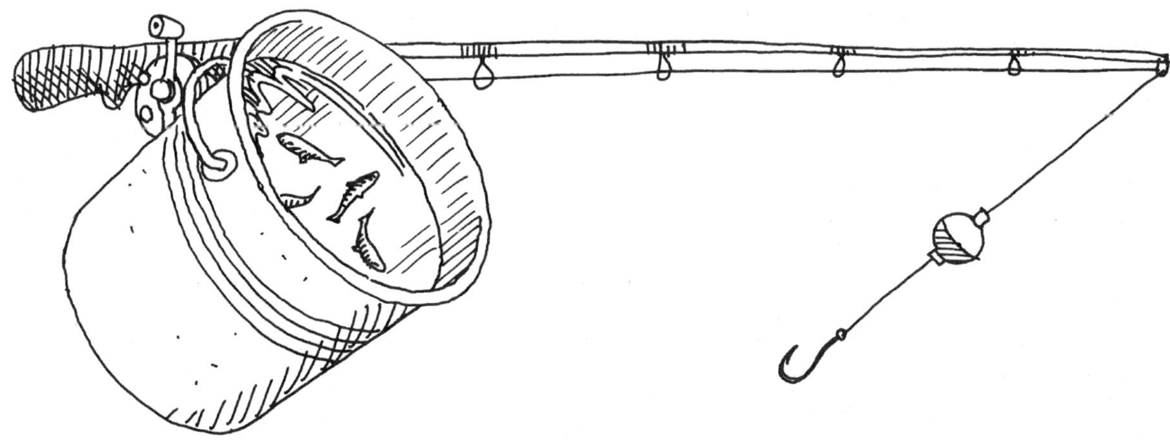

At Home: Think of another reason why Uncle Joe lost his huge fish. Write a paragraph about it.

▶ **Critical Thinking**

Simple Subjects

Underline the simple subject in each sentence. Then use the simple subject and the crossword clues to fill in the puzzle.

1. Our class is studying the human body. (8 Across)
2. The human body is a great machine. (2 Across)
3. The brain works like a switchboard. (2 Down)
4. Body signals go to and from the brain. (5 Down)
5. Our five senses help us learn about the world. (3 Down)
6. Vibrations help us to hear different sounds. (9 Across)
7. The inner ear contains three bones. (7 Across)
8. Tomorrow an eye doctor is coming to speak to us. (1 Down)
9. We are going to experiment with optical illusions. (4 Across)
10. Nutrition will be a topic later in the week. (6 Across)

At Home: Design an exercise program that you can put into action three times a week. Write down your goals. Circle the simple subject in each sentence.

Name________________________________ Date______________ **Extend 9**

Simple Predicates

Read the directions below. Underline the simple predicate in each sentence. Then play the game.

1. Play this game with classmates.
2. Print your name on a sheet of paper.
3. Then exchange papers with classmates.
4. Each player writes a silly sentence.
5. Each word of the sentence starts with a letter in the name.
6. What if you get the name "Bud Jones"?
7. Try the following sentence.
8. "Bertha understood David Jackson owed Ned eight sandwiches."
9. Maybe your name is "Robert Jones."
10. "Rod owed Bert eleven round trips just over night every Sunday."

Della
Don't
eat
lavender
lemons
anytime

At Home: Make up a set of directions for your own game using the predicates you underlined above.

▶ Critical Thinking

Name______________________________ Date______________ **Extend 10**

Combining Sentences: Compound Subjects

Combine each sentence pair by creating a compound subject. Then underline the compound subject in the new sentence.

1. Robert L. Stevenson wrote poetry.
Shel Silverstein wrote poetry.

____

____

2. Lee-Young read "My Shadow."
Ruiz read "My Shadow."

____

____

3. Did Shel Silverstein write "Shoe Talk"?
Did Robert L. Stevenson write "Shoe Talk"?

____

____

4. Limericks are fun to write.
Haiku poems are fun to write.

____

____

5. Sarah will write about Robert L. Stevenson.
Jamie will write about Robert L. Stevenson.

____

____

6. "Mother Doesn't Want a Dog" is my favorite poem.
"Mother's Nerves" is my favorite poem.

____

____

At Home: What two poems or stories do you like? Tell a family member and explain your answer using compound subjects in your sentences.

▶ **Critical Thinking**

Name________________________________ Date______________ **Extend 11**

Combining Sentences: Compound Predicates

First, read all of the sentences. Then choose words from the word box to complete each one. Combine each pair of sentences and then underline the compound predicate.

ate	biked	climb	hiked	fly
photograph	sail	slept	tour	visit

1. Do you want to ________________ France?

Do you want to ________________ France?

____

2. Will you ________________ there?

Will you ________________ there?

____

3. In Paris you can ________________ the Eiffel Tower.

In Paris you can ________________ the Eiffel Tower.

____

4. Mona and her parents ________________ in the countryside.

Mona and her parents ________________ in the countryside.

____

5. They ________________ in an old castle.

They ________________ in an old castle.

____

At Home: Draw a picture of a place you would like to visit and write a caption for your picture using a compound predicate.

▶ **Critical Thinking**

Name________________________________ Date______________ **Extend 12**

Mechanics and Usage: Correcting Run-on Sentences

Boris was writing a report on his computer. Then something went wrong. All of his sentences became run-ons. Correct the run-on sentences and rewrite Boris's report. Use separate sentences, compound sentences, or combine subjects or predicates. See how smooth you can make the writing!

> Benjamin Franklin was born in 1706 in Boston, Massachusetts he had many brothers he had many sisters Ben's father taught him how to make candles he taught him how to make soap the job was not fun for Ben Ben went to work for his brother James in his print shop he learned all about type he learned how to run a printing press after Ben was grown, he opened his own printing shop he married he had two sons William was one son. Francis was one son Francis died of smallpox when he was four Ben published *Poor Richard's Almanack* He invented the Franklin Stove He invented the lightning rod. He . . .

____

____

____

____

____

____

____

____

____

At Home: Underline the complete predicate(s) in the sentences you wrote.

Name____________________ Date__________ **Extend 13**

Mixed Review

Rewrite the following paragraphs with corrections on the lines below. Join some sentences, and separate others. Make sure each sentence has a complete subject and a complete predicate.

Glenna Goodacre is a sculptor she is also a mother and a grandmother. She designed the first coin to honor a Native American woman.

The woman is Sacajawea. A Shoshone guide who went with Lewis and Clark on part of their journey to the Pacific. The coin. Shows Sacajawea carrying her young son he went on the voyage, too.

Can you tell why the coin is very different from others. Sacajawea's face looks out directly at us other coins show people's profiles.

Glenna Goodacre is the first woman ever to design a U.S. coin now isn't that amazing.

____

____

____

____

____

____

____

____

____

____

____

At Home: Look closely at any coin, both the head and tail sides. Write a description of the coin. Use complete sentences and correct punctuation. Show your work to a family member.

▶ **Critical Thinking**

Name ______________________ Date ____________ **Extend 14**

Common Errors: Sentence Fragments and Run-On Sentences

Correct sentence fragments and run-on sentences by rewriting the directions below.

For the Birds

To make a bird feeder. You will need an empty half-gallon milk carton, tape. Scissors, string, and birdseed. Use dish soap and warm water to wash out the carton then dry it with a towel tape the top closed. Cut out. The two sides of the carton, leaving about an inch around the sides. And about two inches along the bottom. Carefully punch two holes in the top of the carton run the string through the holes so that the feeder can hang from a tree branch. Fill the bottom. Of the carton with birdseed. Hang the feeder in a tree be sure to keep it filled up.

____

____

____

____

____

____

____

____

____

____

____

____

At Home: Do some after-school bird watching. Keep notes about the birds that you observe and see if you can identify them. Be sure to use complete sentences in your notes.

▶ Critical Thinking

Name________________________ Date____________ **Extend 15**

Study Skills: Note-Taking and Summarizing

Leandra and Dale are working on a science report on wind. They go to the library and read an article entitled "Blowing over the Earth," which presents important information on their report topic.

Read the article. Then help Leandra and Dale by taking notes about the main idea and supporting details on the note card shown below.

It cools you on a hot day and brings on a chill in winter. It is the earth's breath, which is known as wind. Wind is no more than air in motion. The motion is caused by differences in air temperature and air pressure. The warmth of the sun reflecting off the earth heats the air.

Air is made up of molecules. Heat causes air molecules to rise. As the warmed molecules of air rise, cooler molecules of air rush in to take their place.

The direction of the wind and the speed at which it moves affect our weather. You can tell from which direction the wind is moving by observing a flag or a wind vane.

When weather forecasters tell us "there are west winds," this means that the wind is traveling from west to east.

How do scientists measure the wind's strength and speed? They use the Beaufort Wind Scale, invented by a British admiral over a century ago. This scale helps to demonstrate the strength of the wind. Number 1 indicates a calm wind moving less than 1 mile per hour, like the movement of smoke rising into the sky. Number 12 indicates a destructive wind greater than 73 miles per hour, like the winds in a hurricane.

Main Idea: ____

Supporting details: ____

____

____

____

____

At Home: Use the notes you took on the article about wind and write a summary.

▶ **Critical Thinking**

Name______________________________ Date____________ **Extend 16**

Vocabulary: Time-Order Words

Rearrange the following sentences in good time order.

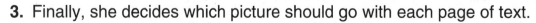

1. Then, she thinks about where the story takes place.
2. When an artist designs a picture book, she does things step by step.
3. Finally, she decides which picture should go with each page of text.
4. Maybe the very last decision is choosing paint or crayon or ink to draw the pictures.
5. As soon as she begins laying out the book, she decides if the picture should show a character close up or far away.
6. Next, she thinks about the characters.
7. First, she reads the story that the author wrote.
8. Perhaps she will choose to show a bird's-eye view, looking down from someplace high.

At Home: Tell a family member how time-order words can help you in speaking and writing.

▶ **Critical Thinking**

Name______________________ Date__________ **Extend 17**

Composition: Main Idea

A. Choose a topic sentence for the supporting details listed below. Write the letter of the sentence on the line.

1. _____ You can visit volcanoes. You can go snorkeling. You can go beach-combing on miles of sandy shore.

a. Outdoor sports are fun.
b. Hawaii is a great vacation spot.
c. Everyone likes going to the beach.

2. _____ It is interesting. It is challenging. It comes in handy for three meals a day!

a. Cooking is a delicious hobby.
b. Learning a foreign language is something everyone should do.
c. There is nothing dull about learning to play an instrument.

3. _____ It is exciting to get a closer look at faraway places, and knowing more about the planets can tell us more about how the universe began.

a. Photographs of Jupiter show its moons.
b. Space exploration can help us understand our past.
c. Mercury is the closest planet to the sun.

4. _____ It includes Lake Tahoe, a year-round vacation spot, and Mt. Whitney, the tallest peak in the continental U.S.

a. The Sierra Nevada is a good place for mountain climbing.
b. The Sierra Nevada is a paradise for skiers.
c. The Sierra Nevada extends down the eastern side of California.

5. _____ It is famous for its hills, its cable cars, Fisherman's Wharf, sourdough bread, the Golden Gate Bridge, and the Forty-Niners.

a. San Francisco is a distinctive city.
b. San Francisco has a beautiful skyline.
c. The Bay Bridge connects San Francisco to Oakland.

B. Look at the picture of the Statue of Liberty.
Write a topic sentence and two supporting details about it.

____

____

Name________________________ Date____________ **Extend 18**

Nouns

Write each word from the box under the correct heading in the chart.

actor	Asia	bamboo	wrestler	chopsticks
emperor	fan	kite	island	Japan
Kyoto	lantern	puppeteer	rice	sandals
samurai	lord	tea	Tokyo	kimono
	yen		cherry-blossoms	

Nouns

PERSON	PLACE	THING

At Home: Think of other words that you could add to the chart. Explain why they belong where they do.

▶ **Critical Thinking**

Name______________________________ Date_____________ **Extend 19**

Singular and Plural Nouns

Each answer to the puzzle is a plural noun. To complete the puzzle, add *s* or *es* to the nouns in the word box.

acorn	branch	bush	finch	flower
pea	radish	reed	syrup	weed

Across

1. Seeds are formed here.
2. These are the woody parts of a tree that grow from the trunk.
5. These are made from sap.
8. These are unwanted plants.

Down

1. These are birds.
2. These are shrubs.
3. Squirrels store them.
4. These are grasses that grow in wet places.
6. These are vegetables with a sharp taste.
7. These come from pods.

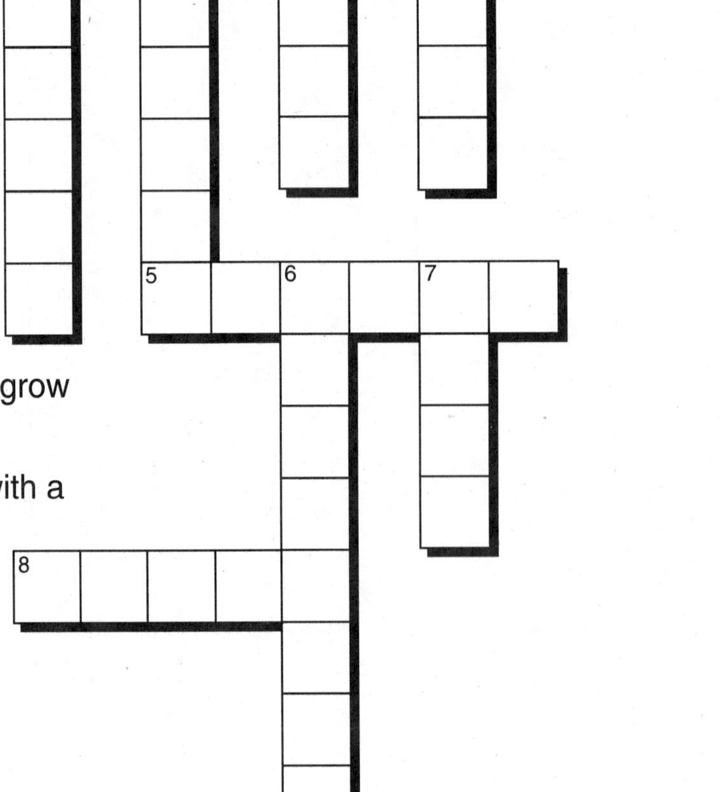

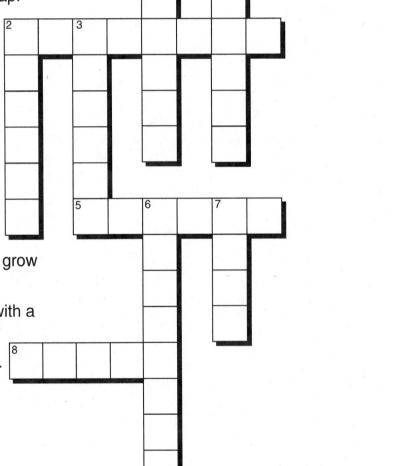

At Home: Make up your own crossword puzzle or word search using the words in the word box.

Name________________________ Date____________ **Extend 20**

Nouns ending with *y*

Write the plural noun that describes each picture.

1. 

____

2. 

____

3. 

____

4. 

____

5. 

____

6. 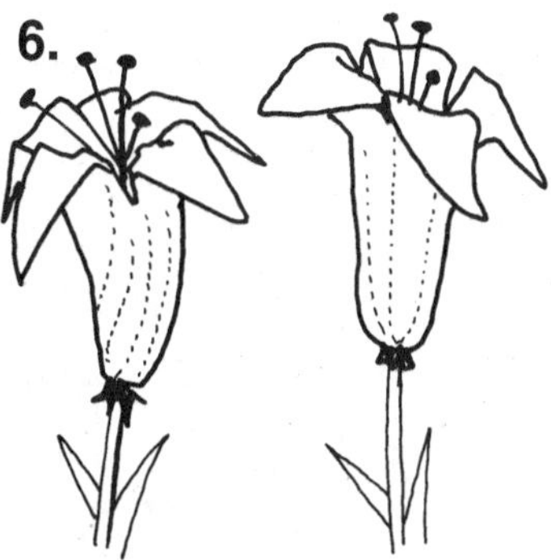

____

7. 

____

8. 

____

9. 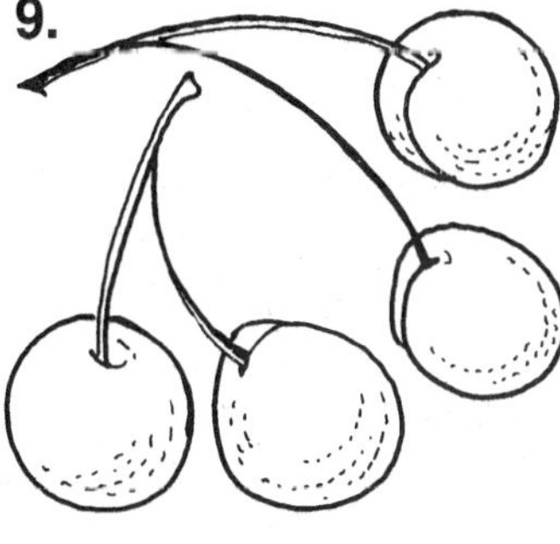

____

At Home: Think of your own plural noun. Draw a picture of the word. Ask a family member to identify it.

▶ **Critical Thinking**

Name________________________ Date__________ **Extend 21**

More Plural Nouns

To complete the puzzle, write the plural noun of the following words.

Across	Down
3. scissors	**1.** deer
6. mouse	**2.** moose
8. woman	**4.** child
9. ox	**5.** sheep
10. tooth	**7.** man

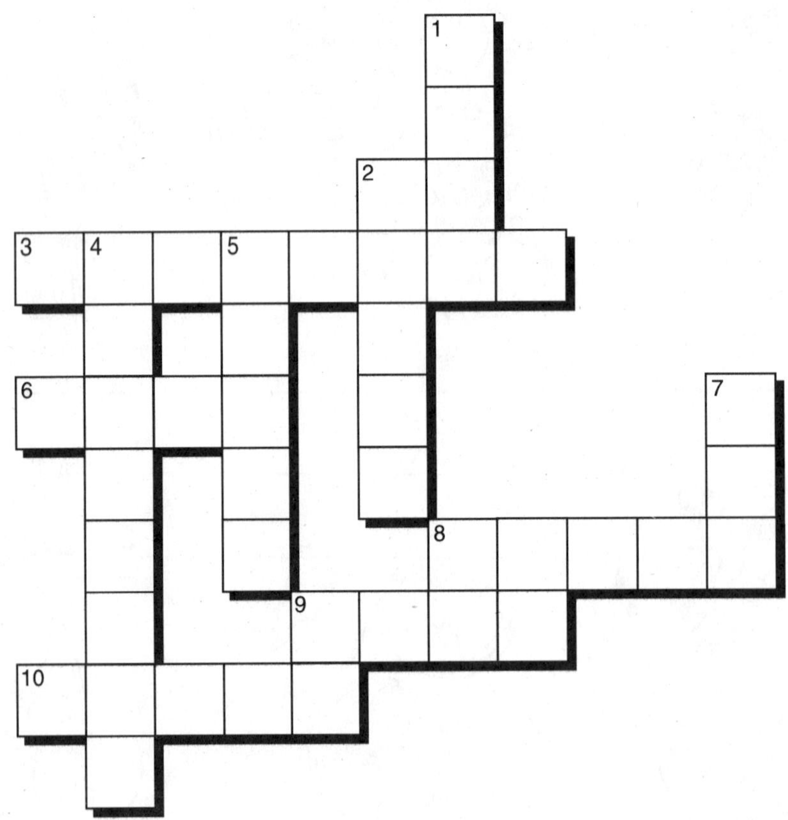

At Home: How many of the plural nouns in this puzzle keep the same spelling as the singular form of the noun?

Common and Proper Nouns

Correct the following invitation, memo, poster, and schedule. Underline letters that should be capitalized with three lines. (b)

Come to a party
for
brenda milkens
friday, july 7, 2000
8:00 P. M.

lincoln park zoo
special event

gorilla house opening

entertainment
food games
memorial day
may 29
Rain date: june 3

MEMO

From: jim bennett
Re: Meeting next thurs.

I got your note last week. Sorry I can't come to the meeting next thursday. I'll be in chicago at a sales meeting.

Leave		Arrive	
detroit	9:00 P.M.	kansas city	11:00 P.M.
grand rapids	7:00 A.M.	milwaukee	8:00 A.M.
st. clare shores	6:00 P.M.	new york	11:30 P.M.

At Home: Design a poster to advertise an upcoming school event.

Name_______________________ Date_____________ **Extend 23**

Mechanics and Usage: Capitalization

Pretend you are Doreen and you wrote this letter to your grandmother. Add capital letters where they belong.

Dear granny:

I can't wait till we come see you on thanksgiving. My teacher, miss robinson, showed us how to make turkeys with apples and toothpicks. I made one for you.

mister phillips asked me to walk his dog sparkles next saturday and Sunday. he is taking a trip to california. He wants to visit yosemite national park and knott's berry farm.

Dad took me to doctor driller last monday after school. I didn't have any cavities. Hooray! Then dad drove me down mulberry street. The cattail nature center was open. We saw bees in a hive. miss fremont gave a talk about how honey is made.

I must study for my english test tomorrow. I just finished reading *little house in the big woods*, by laura ingalls wilder.

love,

doreen

At Home: Substitute new proper nouns for those used in the letter above.

Name________________________________ Date______________ **Extend 24**

Mixed Review

A. Name each picture in each pair. Write both singular and plural nouns.

1.  

______________________ ______________________

2.  

______________________ ______________________

3. 

______________________ ______________________

B. Underline the proper nouns on the following calendar book and address book.

Calendar Book

February holidays:
Groundhog Day
My Birthday
Valentine's Day
Presidents' Day

Address Book

My dentist
Dr. D. Beadley
1765 East Milford Ave.
Sharon, CT 06069
860-555-5555
My lawyer
Sara Brentwell
345 College Ave.
Essex, VT 05452
878-555-5555

At Home: List all the names and addresses of five different friends or relatives. Use correct punctuation. These listings can be part of your personal address book, if you wish.

▶ **Critical Thinking**

Name________________________________ Date______________ **Extend 25**

Singular Possessive Nouns

Rewrite the paragraph. Use singular possessive nouns to replace the underlined fragments. Remember to include an apostrophe.

The Tale of Michael

I found the joke book that belongs to Jake at the house of my grandfather. The cane that belongs to my grandfather was left at the country store that belongs to Clem. Clem came to our house in the car that belongs to his mother and left the cane and a frozen pizza from the deli that is owned by Pino. I returned the joke book to Jake and borrowed a CD that belongs to his sister. Jake asked to borrow the radio that belongs to my older brother. My brother said he needed the radio to take to his job on the farm belonging to Dutton. Mom said that the corn from last week was sweet and delicious.

____

____

____

____

____

____

____

____

At Home: Describe a country scene. Use singular and possessive nouns.

Name________________________________ Date______________ **Extend** 26

Plural Possessive Nouns

Mark an X on each plural possessive noun that is not written correctly. Then write each word correctly on the lines at the bottom of the page.

Dear Diary:

Yesterday, Amy and I took five three-year-olds to the playground. Two boys pretended to be super-heroes. The boys yelling made me hold my ears. Three girls had a fight over some cement trucks. I dried two of the girls tears and suggested how the three of them could play together. Finally, they were happy.

Then two small dogs came running and barking around the kids kickball game. The dogs barking stopped the game. The dogs owners came running onto the field. "We are sorry," they said. "Our four-year-old removed the pooches leashes from their collars."

At snack time, three older kids spilled their juice right onto two boys sweaters. The boys tears flowed this time. We wiped off the juice, and all was A-OK once again. What a tiring day!

1. ____________________ 5. ____________________
2. ____________________ 6. ____________________
3. ____________________ 7. ____________________
4. ____________________ 8. ____________________

At Home: Do you think the writer of this diary entry enjoys volunteering? Tell why or why not.

▶ **Critical Thinking**

Name________________________________ Date______________ **Extend 27**

Combining Sentences: Nouns

Complete the following old tale. Use compound subjects and compound objects. Remember to use *and* or *or*.

One day John ______________________________ stole a pig from their neighbors Bess ______________________________. They took the pig home. ______________________________ looked out the window and saw ______________________________ coming. Quickly John put the pig in a crib. John got out a blanket ______________________________. He put it on the pig. He waited for ______________________________.

"What is the matter with the baby, John?" Bess asked.

"The baby has measles ______________________________," said John. You cannot see him. The doctor said the measles will go inside the baby. The doctor said this would make the baby turn pink."

Bess ______________________________ stared at the crib.

Then ______________________________ reached down and uncovered the baby.

"Don't blame me if the baby turned into a pig," said John.

"I will take the pig home," said Bess. "I will take good care of the pig."

"Oink!" said the pig.

At Home: Write a title for this folk tale.

Name________________________ Date____________ **Extend 28**

Mechanics and Usage: Abbreviations

Use abbreviations to complete a February school calendar. Write the name of the month and abbreviate the days of the week. Add entries with abbreviations for each day shown below.

Feb. 4: Meet with Mister Collins 3:30
9: Governor McDonald visits Grades 5–6
11: Doctor Hernandez visits Grade 3
14: School closed for Presidents' Day
23: Grade 3 visits Senator Smith
24: River Street Conservation Society meeting 5:30
29: Chess Club plans April contest

____

______	______	______	______	______	______	______
		1	2	3	4	5
6	7	8	9	10	11	12
13	14	15	16	17	18	19
20	21	22	23	24	25	26
27	28	29				

At Home: Why are calendars important to us? Write a few sentences to explain your answer.

▶ **Critical Thinking**

Name________________________ Date____________ **Extend 29**

Mixed Review

A. Combine the following sentences. Underline the nouns in each new sentence.

1. I will send a letter to my teacher. I will send a letter to the insect expert.

____

2. We will find out about ticks. We will find out about insects.

____

B. There was a computer glitch, and this insect expert's letter needs some fixing. Commas and capitals and other punctuation need to be added. Correct the grammar mistakes. Watch out for possessive nouns!

natural history museum
New York, Ny 10023
Jan 5, 2004

Ms liz Randolph
467 Clinton ave.
Carrboro, NC 17510

Dear Liz,

Your brothers argument is the correct one. A tick is not an insect. A ticks eight legs is a big clue. This makes it an arthropod, just like a spider. A tick has no wings, but an insect does. Ticks bodies are short and round without any segments. An insects body has three distinct parts. A wood tick is very tiny. It lives in the woods. It sucks the blood of deer and other animals. When the tick has not eaten, its body is flat, soft, and elastic. After it has eaten, its body swells.

Some ticks carry disease so don't handle them. If you have a pet that gets ticks, take it to a veterinarian. He or she will know what to do.

sincerely,
Jeremy douglas

At Home: Write sentences about insects. Use compound subjects such as *ticks and mites.* Share your work with a family member.

Name________________________ Date__________ **Extend 30**

Common Errors: Plurals and Possessives

Read the letter below. Rewrite the letter, correcting the mistakes made with plural nouns and possessive nouns.

Dear Aunt Bess,

Thank you for sending me the easel and paint's. I have already painted three watercolor's, and I am working on another. One is of a birds nest in the tree outside my moms' office window. I also have signed up for some arts' and craft's classes' at the Childrens' Museum. My teachers husband is going to set up weekend art workshop's, and my friends' and I might be able to take them. Plus, our next door neighbors studio is mine to use while she is out of town. Your gift's will help me find success with all of these activitie's!

Your's truly,
Terry

At Home: When have you received a special gift? Write a thank-you note to a relative. Be sure to punctuate plural nouns and plural possessives correctly.

▶ **Critical Thinking**

Name________________________________ Date______________ **Extend 31**

Study Skills: Parts of a Book

Althea loved information and often researched topics that interested her. Her last research topic was sound and light energy. She kept note cards and organized them by the pages of books on which she found the information. Unfortunately, Althea's new puppy knocked the piles of cards off of her bed. Now they are all mixed up on the floor of her room.

Help Althea organize her cards into these five categories: **title page, copyright page, table of contents, index,** and **glossary.** Write where they belong on the lines.

1. copyright © 1999 ______________
2. by Anita Pohwerz, Ph.D. ______________
3. Sound Waves 4–7, 18 ______________
4. Chapter 3 What Makes a Rainbow? .... 19 ______________
5. reflection [ri-flek-shən] the return of light or sound waves from a surface ______________
6. Chapter 1 Waves of Energy............... 3 ______________
7. lux [ləks] a unit of measure for the brightness of light ______________
8. The Book of Energy ______________
9. wave [wāv] a disturbance that travels through matter or space ______________
10. Science Publishing Company, Inc.
San Franciso • Chicago • Boston ______________
11. Rainbows 19–25, 27, 42 ______________
12. Index.............116 ______________
13. Neon 67–72
with laser production 70 ______________
14. Chapter 12 Problems of Noise Pollution.......88 ______________
15. pitch [pich] the highness or lowness of a sound ______________

At Home: Make up another card for each pile of Althea's cards.

Vocabulary: Compound Words

Each answer to the crossword puzzle is a compound word. Can you figure out its theme?

Across

1. The shining light of the sun
3. He predicts the weather.
4. They fall from the sky.
6. You can get this when you're at the beach.
7. Every one has six points but no two are exactly alike.
8. You wear it to keep from getting wet.
9. This warns ships of fog.

Down

1. A fall of snow
2. He usually has a carrot nose.
5. A sudden, heavy rain
7. The light of the sun

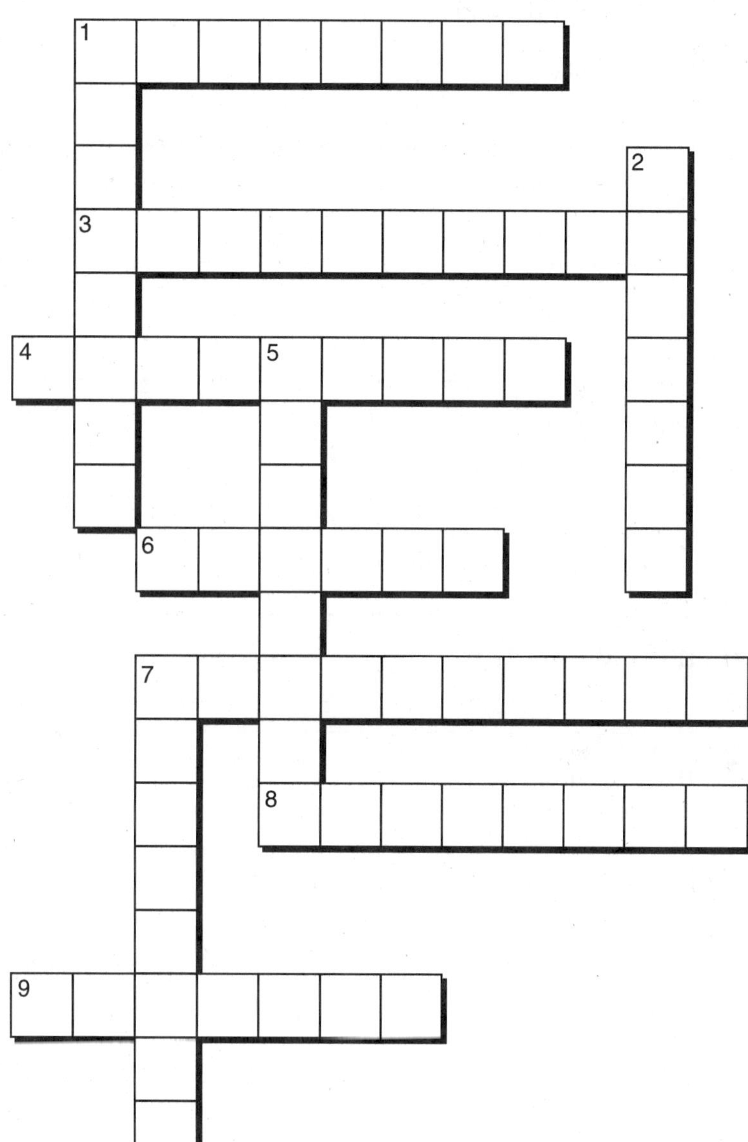

At Home: List other compound words relating to the theme above and create your own crossword puzzle with them.

▶ **Critical Thinking**

Name________________________ Date____________ **Extend 33**

Composition Skills: Writing Descriptions

Use vivid details and words that appeal to the five senses to write a sentence that describes each thing below. Be sure your sentence creates a clear mental picture.

1. a cold day

____

2. a strong wind

____

3. a new bicycle

____

4. bright moonlight

____

5. a glowing sunset

____

6. a busy airport

____

7. a traffic jam

____

8. a jolly baby

____

9. a friendly dog

____

10. students in a quiet classroom

____

11. students in a cafeteria

____

12. a boat on a lake

____

At Home: How does the weather affect your mood? Write a description of the weather and include details about how it makes you feel.

▶ **Critical Thinking**

Name________________________________ Date______________ **Extend 34**

Action Verbs

What kind of jokes did Albert Einstein, the great scientist, make?

To find the answer, write the action verb in each sentence. Then unscramble the circled letters and write them on the lines below.

1. Bill often works late into the night. ◯_ _◯_
2. He illustrates children's books. ◯_ _ _ _ _ _ _ _ _ _
3. Sometimes he paints with a tiny brush. _ _ _ _ _◯
4. Often he mixes several colors together. _ _ _◯_
5. Bill also carves wood. ◯◯_ _ _ _
6. He designs totem poles and Kachina dolls. _ _ _ _ _ _ _
7. He decorates them with Indian symbols. _ _◯_◯_ _ _ _
8. Sometimes he sells his artwork. _ _ _ _ _
9. He often exhibits his work in a museum. _ _ _ _ _ _ _ _
10. Sometimes he visits children in schools. _ _ _ _ _◯

_ _ _ _ _ _ _ _ _ _

At Home: Work with a family member. Form at least two more action verbs with the circled letters. *Ski* is one possibility.

▶ **Critical Thinking**

Name______________________________ Date______________ **Extend 35**

Verb Tenses

Rewrite the sentences from the following paragraph in the correct time order—past, present, and future.

My album is almost full. That will be great! Maybe someday I will take a photography class. When I was younger, I loved to look at photos of me as a baby. I enjoy taking pictures of my friends. Snap, snap, my camera goes. Everyone says I was a cutie pie! When I am older, I will take pictures of places I visit. I will learn how to develop my own film. Now I have my own camera.

1. ______________________________
2. ______________________________
3. ______________________________
4. ______________________________
5. ______________________________
6. ______________________________
7. ______________________________
8. ______________________________
9. ______________________________
10. ______________________________

At Home: Do you have a favorite photograph in your family album? Write a story about it.

Name____________________ Date__________ **Extend 36**

Subject-Verb Agreement

Olga recently arrived from Europe. She is learning English fast, but has some difficulty with verb tenses. She wrote the following in her diary after a tough day. Help Olga. Cross out the incorrect verb and write the correct verb form above it.

Dear Diary,

This week's math problems takes a lot of time. Steven and Jesse works the number problems together. Joan figure out the solutions all by herself.

"Can we calculate on the calculator?" I asks.

Miss Fernandez say, "No, use your brains, not a machine."

My pals, Jenna and Fred, offers to help me. We arrives at the wrong answer. Miss Fernandez explain what we did wrong. We think and think and finally solves it. The recess bells rings and away we go!

I hopes tomorrow is a better day.

At Home: Locate a country in Europe on a map and list three of its cities and two of its rivers.

Name________________________________ Date______________ **Extend 37**

Spelling Present-Tense and Past-Tense Verbs

Complete the puzzle by writing the verb tense shown in parentheses in the puzzle. Use the puzzle clue.

I (hurry)	(past)	**4 across**	I (whisper)	(present)	**3 down**
You (scurry)	(past)	**2 down**	You (shop)	(past)	**5 down**
We (try)	(past)	**9 across**	They (ship)	(past)	**5 across**
She (wonder)	(present)	**6 across**	We (plop)	(past)	**7 down**
He (yell)	(present)	**1 across**	You (drop)	(past)	**8 across**

At Home: Make up a poem using words in the puzzle. Recite your poem to a family member.

Name________________________________ Date____________ **Extend 38**

Mechanics and Usage: Commas in a Series

Pretend your younger brother or sister wrote the following report for class. He or she asked you to proofread it. Read the paragraphs and add commas where needed.

Do you know what the closest star to Earth is? Yes it is the sun. All the other stars are very far away. Some of the brightest "stars" are actually planets. Venus Mars Jupiter and Saturn can be seen without a telescope. There are red stars yellow stars white stars and blue-white stars. Blue-white stars are the hottest the red stars are the coolest and the others are in between.

Most constellations are named after animals ancient gods or heroes. See if you can find Orion Taurus the Bull and the Big Dipper in a book. Then share your information with your parents a brother a sister or a friend.

____

____

____

____

____

____

____

____

At Home: Draw a picture of one of the constellations named above. Then tell a family member about it.

Name__________ Date__________ **Extend 39**

Mixed Review

A. Write the correct verb tenses as indicated in the parentheses. Then write a sentence with the verb. **Challenge:** Try to keep your sentences on one topic, such as art or sports.

1. jump (past) __________
2. practice (future) __________
3. pasted (present) __________
4. create (past) __________
5. hurry (past) __________
6. watch (past) __________
7. stop (past) __________
8. carried (future) __________
9. will try (past) __________
10. grin (past) __________

B. Rewrite each sentence. Add a verb and commas where they belong.

11. I ______ to the sixth-grade class the kids in the library and our principal.

____

____

12. Everyone said we ______ soap towels wax and a hose for the car wash.

____

____

13. Let's ______ if we can hold it on one of the following dates: Saturday the seventh, the fourteenth, or the twenty-first.

____

____

At Home: Observe a family member in the kitchen preparing food. List as many verbs as you can that describe the action being done. For example: *cook, mixing, marinated.*

▶ **Critical Thinking**

Name________________________________ Date______________ **Extend 40**

Main Verbs and Helping Verbs

Pretend you are a reporter for your school newspaper. You are covering the orchestra rehearsal and taking notes. Locate and write each helping verb and main verb below. Then draw one line under the helping verb and draw two lines under each main verb.

The school orchestra is rehearsing in the auditorium. Mr. Ames will conduct the concert tonight. I can hear the strings. The violinist is making a squeaky sound. The boy playing cello is humming with the music. A girl with her flute is running toward her seat. The trumpet and trombone players were talking a second ago. Mr. Ames is tapping his baton. I bet he will scold them.

"You should arrive on time," he said to the girl.

"Boys, I will need quiet," he said.

I shall attend the concert with my parents. My cousin Ted would enjoy the music, I think. I could ask him to join us. I will write my review for the school newspaper tomorrow morning.

1. ____________	6. ____________	11. ____________
2. ____________	7. ____________	12. ____________
3. ____________	8. ____________	13. ____________
4. ____________	9. ____________	14. ____________
5. ____________	10. ____________	15. ____________

At Home: What musical instrument do you play or would like to play? Write about it using main and helping verbs.

▶ **Critical Thinking**

Name____________________________ Date____________ **Extend 41**

Using Helping Verbs

Here is a riddle: What travels around the world but stays in a corner?

To find the answer, first circle the helping verb and the main verb in each sentence. Then unscramble the underlined letters. Write each letter on a line below.

1. When I was your age, I had received my share of bumps and bruises.
2. On the soccer field, my big toe was stepped on.
3. The doctor had looked at an X-ray; it was only a bruise.
4. One day, I was running on the sidewalk.
5. Then oops! I realized I had tripped and cut my knee.
6. I had walked around with a bandage for a week.
7. For years, Dad and my uncle were trying to get me to believe that a gorilla came to visit me when I was two.
8. I have never believed those jokers!
9. When I was five, I told Mom that an elephant had smashed my broken toy.
10. Kids have swapped stories like that for generations.

___   ___ ___ ___ ___ ___

At Home: Make up a riddle. Tell it to a family member.

Name______________________________ Date____________ **Extend 42**

Linking Verbs

Read each sentence. Underline the linking verb. Circle the noun or adjective in the predicate. Then replace the noun or adjective with a synonym.

1. Our class is excited. ______________________________
2. Our spring play will be funny. ______________________________
3. The characters in it are silly. ______________________________
4. Samantha is the narrator. ______________________________
5. My best pal, Mohammed, is tall. ______________________________
6. Deciding who plays the giant was easy. ______________________________
7. The stage in the auditorium is huge. ______________________________
8. Carrie says her stomach is jumpy. ______________________________
9. I am not nervous. ______________________________
10. I am the one who pulls the curtains. ______________________________
11. The curtains are shiny. ______________________________
12. Our teacher is proud of us. ______________________________
13. Our parents are happy. ______________________________

At Home: Write a short description of a scene for a class play. Include linking verbs.

▶ **Critical Thinking**

Name________________________________ Date____________ **Extend 43**

Using Linking Verbs

Add the correct form of the verb *be* to each sentence. Then find and circle all the forms of the verb *be* in the puzzle below. Look down, across, and diagonally.

Family Fun

Every year during the summer our family members ____________________ guests at a reunion. Last year there ____________________ about 75 people. The kids ____________________ different ages, from tiny babies to teens. My cousin Jean ____________________ the oldest. I ____________________ in between her and the babies. I ____________________ twelve on my last birthday. Everyone ____________________ always busy doing something. The grown-ups did a lot of talking and cooking. The kids played games. The biggest event ____________________ the family baseball game. My team won. We ____________________ all so proud! I wonder where our next reunion ____________________.

w	e	r	e	a	m
a	i	a	m	r	y
m	i	i	i	e	w
a	m	s	i	i	a
s	m	s	a	b	r
a	i	a	a	r	e

McGraw-Hill School Division

At Home: Make up your own word search puzzle with words from the above paragraph. Have a family member solve it.

▶ **Critical Thinking**

Irregular Verbs

Use the irregular forms of the verbs in parentheses to complete each sentence.

1. I (eat) ____________________ a snack after school.

2. Then I (go) ____________________ to my art class at the recreation center.

3. I (bring) ____________________ along some of my favorite paintings.

4. I (make) ____________________ one using crayon and watercolors.

5. "Have you (see) ____________________ Max's picture?" Mrs. Applebaum asked everyone. "It's wonderful."

6. Maria quietly (run) ____________________ into the classroom, trying to be unnoticed.

7. Of course, Ms. Applebaum (see) ____________________ her.

8. She (do) ____________________ not say anything to Maria.

9. She just (give) ____________________ her a stern look.

10. "I had (make) ____________________ some slides to show you last week," said my teacher.

11. "I had (go) ____________________ to the library to borrow some books."

12. "I (come) ____________________ across this book on the Impressionists, and I want to share it with you, too."

At Home: Write a paragraph that continues the story told above. Use irregular verbs in each sentence.

▶ **Critical Thinking**

Name ______________________ Date ____________ **Extend 45**

More Irregular Verbs

A. Complete the chart.

Present Tense	Past Tense	With Have/Had
begin	____________	____________
bring	____________	____________
draw	____________	____________
drive	____________	____________
fly	____________	____________
grow	____________	____________
ride	____________	____________

B. What other irregular verbs might you add to the chart? List them.

____________ ____________ ____________

____________ ____________ ____________

____________ ____________ ____________

At Home: Play a game with a family member. Start by saying a word from the chart above. Then say, "Name its irregular verb when used with *have* or *had*." The family member answers. Continue by taking turns.

▶ **Critical Thinking**

Mechanics and Usage: Contractions with *Not*

Replace two words in each sentence to form a contraction with *not.* Write the new sentence on the lines below.

I do not know what to do for the science fair this year. I have not one clue! If I had not wasted time by talking on the phone to my friend, I may have been further along. I will not do what I did last year. I made an electric circuit that would not work when I set it up. The battery was not working properly.

My parents are not helping me this year. They are not being mean. They just think I need to do it myself. I could not find a book about telescopes. The librarian said she does not know what happened to it. So now I can learn how to make shadow puppets. Do not you think that is a good idea?

At Home: Write a paragraph describing a recent science project. Use contractions.

▶ **Critical Thinking**

Name____________________ Date__________ **Extend 47**

Mixed Review

Add the missing verb to each sentence. Then tell what kind of verb you wrote by writing either *action, linking, helping,* or *irregular.*

A. 1. I __________ a good cook. __________

2. I went to the store and __________ some chicken legs.

____

3. I __________ the clerk five dollars. __________

4. Then I __________ some yellow rice. __________

5. I __________ the chicken with barbecue sauce. __________

6. Mom and Dad __________ on their way home. __________

7. My brother Pablo __________ to make the salad. __________

8. I __________ the vegetables for him. __________

9. Now he __________ the oil, vinegar, and garlic for the salad dressing. __________

10. "You __________ made us very happy," said Mom and Dad.

____

B. Underline all the past-tense verbs in the sentences above.

C. On a separate sheet of paper, write a letter to a friend or relative. Explain how to prepare your favorite recipe. Try to include the four kinds of verbs in your writing.

At Home: Find a recipe in a family cookbook. List all the verbs you find in it, and then write what kind of verb each one is. Share your work with a family member.

▶ **Critical Thinking**

Name________________________________ Date____________ **Extend** 48

Common Errors: Subject-Verb Agreement

A. Pretend you are a newspaper editor. Read the article below. Underline the correct form of the verbs to complete the article.

Bike Expo Next Week

The City and County Safety Committee (is/are) holding a Bicycle Expo. People (bring/brings) their bikes to the mall parking lot on the second Saturday of the month. Volunteers from local agencies (teach/teaches) riders traffic laws. They also (cover/covers) safety rules.

Bike Universe (has/have) donated helmets to the first 15 bicyclists who (come/comes). The bicyclist who (ride/rides) the farthest to get to the expo (receive/receives) a special award. Children under 10 (compete/competes) for t-shirts, streamers, and other prizes. Afternoon activities (include/includes) workshops and races.

Did you know that bike accidents (send/sends) hundreds of children to the hospital every year? However, the Bike Expo (aim/aims) to reduce the number of accidents and serious injuries that (happen/happens) during the summer months by educating people. The scouts from Troop 751 (provide/provides) refreshments. Families (is/are) encouraged to attend.

B. What other events would you plan for a Bike Expo? Write your ideas to add to the article above. Make sure your subjects and verbs agree in each sentence.

____

____

____

____

At Home: What are some bike safety tips that you follow? Write a list of bike safety rules. Be sure that your subjects and verbs agree.

▶ **Critical Thinking**

Name________________________________ Date______________ **Extend 49**

Study Skills: Card Catalog

Fourth-graders at Whitman Elementary School in New York have created a library with books they have written themselves.

1. Fill in the author and subject cards below for a nonfiction book about bridges by Cynthia Hernandez with the title *How the Brooklyn Bridge Was Built.* This book was illustrated. In 1999 it was published by the Whitman School Press. It has 23 pages, and its call number is 624 H.

author card

624
H

________, Cynthia.
How the Brooklyn Bridge
Was Built.
________: Whitman
School Press, © ____.
23 p.: illus.

subject card

___
H

BRIDGES
Hernandez, Cynthia.
____
____
New York: ___________
___________, © 1999.
__ p.: ______________

2. Name other possible subject card headings for this book.

____

3. Make up another book title which might also have a "BRIDGES" subject card.

____

4. Under what letter would you file this book's title card? ______________

At Home: Make up a set of cards (author, subject, and title) for a book you would one day like to write.

Name________________________________ Date______________ **Extend** 50

Vocabulary: Prefixes

Add a prefix from the box to each underlined word to make the sentence make sense.

dis	in	mis	over	pre	re	un

Understanding the Game

Our opponents ______________ understood how tough we could be. We were not as ______________ organized as they thought. We did have ______________ game jitters, but we got over them. We were able to ______________ group and get the job done.

Our coach was ______________ joyed with our playing. He said that before the game, he was ______________ sure we had enough desire to win. But he ______________ considered that idea quickly.

I thought I would be ______________ lucky and just have to sit on the bench. I was ______________ correct. I ended up hitting two runs, which I thought I was ______________ capable of doing. You just never know!

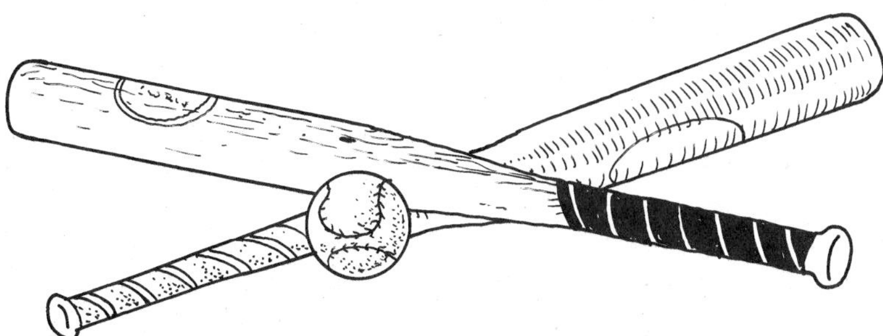

At Home: Define *nonfiction* and *nonexistent.* Then find and define two other words that begin with the prefix *non.*

▶ **Critical Thinking**

Name ______________________ Date ____________ **Extend 51**

Composition: Leads and Endings

Write a strong lead sentence and a strong ending sentence for each topic shown below.

1. A Puppy in the House

Lead ______________________________

Ending ______________________________

2. Moving to a New Neighborhood

Lead ______________________________

Ending ______________________________

3. My Favorite Movie

Lead ______________________________

Ending ______________________________

4. After-School Sports

Lead ______________________________

Ending ______________________________

5. Taking a Trip

Lead ______________________________

Ending ______________________________

6. Doing Volunteer Work

Lead ______________________________

Ending ______________________________

At Home: Can you think of an after-school job? Make up a flyer that describes your services. Be sure you have a strong lead to grab your readers' attention and strong ending to leave them with a good impression!

Name_______________________________ Date______________ **Extend 52**

Adjectives

Use adjectives from the word box to complete the sentences and the puzzle.

easy	equal	huge	neat
old	stormy	strange	young

Across

1. It was a ________________ night with heavy rains.

4. Don't you agree that elephants are not small but ____________________?

6. Stewart just cleaned his room, so it is ____________________ and orderly.

7. 6 + 10 and 9 + 7 are ____________________.

Down

1. I just learned about the ____________________ behavior of puffer fish.

2. The ____________________ man had lived on his farm for ninety years.

3. Did you know that a kid is a ____________________ goat?

5. It is ____________________ to learn how to use a computer.

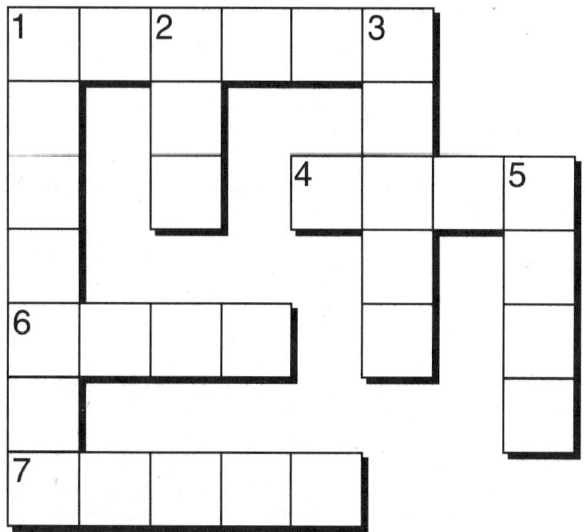

McGraw-Hill School Division

At Home: Use one sentence above as the beginning of a story. Tell your story to a family member.

▶ **Critical Thinking**

Name ______________________ Date ____________ **Extend 53**

Articles: *a, an, the*

A. Write *a, an,* or *the* on the lines to complete the sayings or proverbs.

1. ______________ apple a day keeps the doctor away.
2. ______________ apple doesn't fall far from the tree.
3. ______________ bad workman always blames his tools.
4. Beauty is in ______________ eye of the beholder.
5. ______________ best things come in small packages.
6. The bigger they are, ______________ harder they fall.
7. Birds of ______________ feather flock together.
8. You can't tell ______________ book by its cover.
9. Feed ______________ cold and starve ______________ fever.
10. Let ______________ buyer beware.
11. When ______________ cat is away, ______________ mice will play.
12. Every cloud has ______________ silver lining.
13. Curiosity killed ______________ cat.
14. ______________ early bird catches the worm.
15. Early to bed and early to rise, makes ______________ man healthy, wealthy, and wise.

B. Choose one proverb above and explain its meaning in your own words.

____

____

____

At Home: Ask a parent to share his or her favorite proverb with you. Then illustrate the proverb with a drawing.

Name________________________________ Date______________ **Extend 54**

Adjectives After Linking Verbs

Pretend you were driving in the country and came across a farmer's vegetable stand. The farmer displayed signs to encourage you to buy his goods.

Read the signs. Circle the linking verbs. Underline the adjectives that describe the foods.

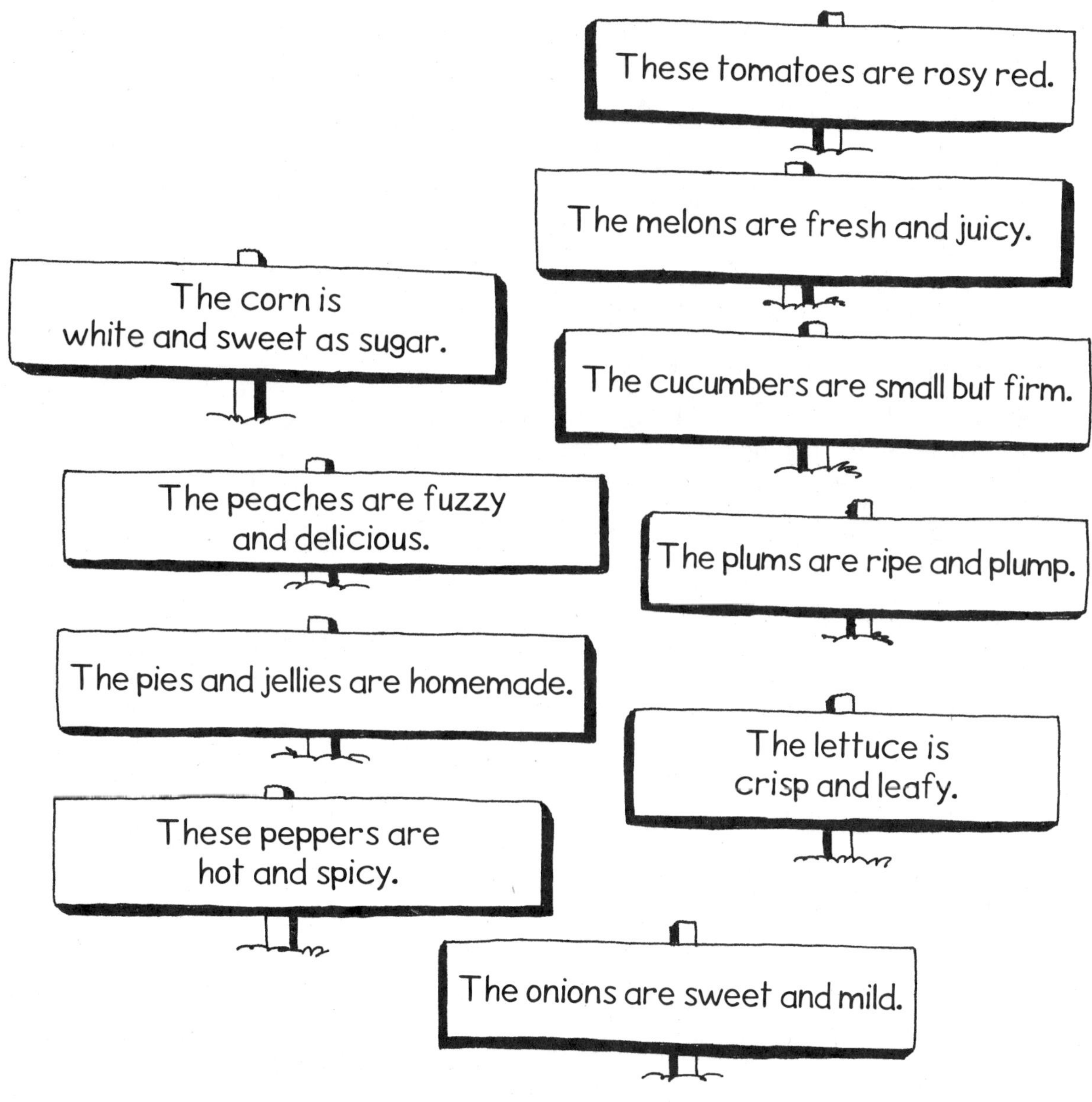

These tomatoes are rosy red.
The melons are fresh and juicy.
The corn is white and sweet as sugar.
The cucumbers are small but firm.
The peaches are fuzzy and delicious.
The plums are ripe and plump.
The pies and jellies are homemade.
The lettuce is crisp and leafy.
These peppers are hot and spicy.
The onions are sweet and mild.

At Home: Pretend you bought five different foods and tasted them all. Write five sentences that use *was* and *were* to describe what you ate.

▶ **Critical Thinking**

Name______________________________ Date____________ **Extend 55**

Mechanics and Usage: Proper Adjectives

Read each sentence and underline the proper adjective. Write it correctly on the line. Then color the flag appropriately.

1. The spanish flag has a red stripe on both the bottom and top of the flag. It has a wider yellow stripe or band in the center.

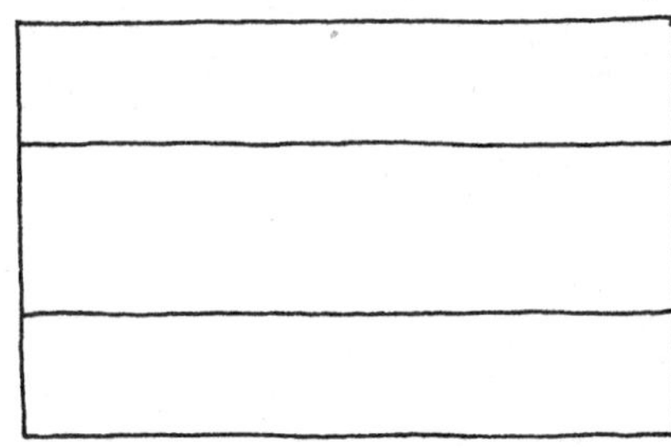

____

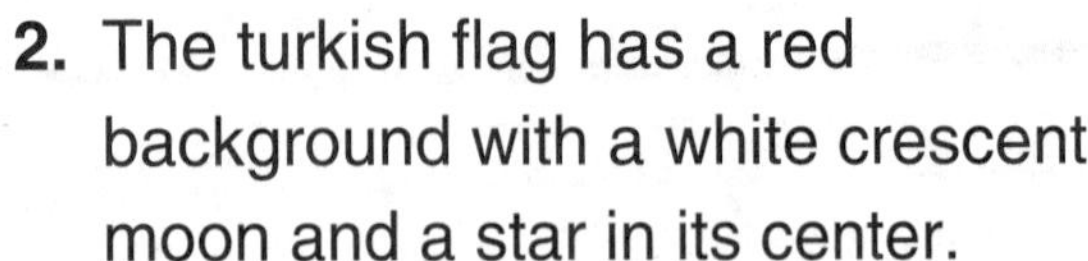

2. The turkish flag has a red background with a white crescent moon and a star in its center.

____

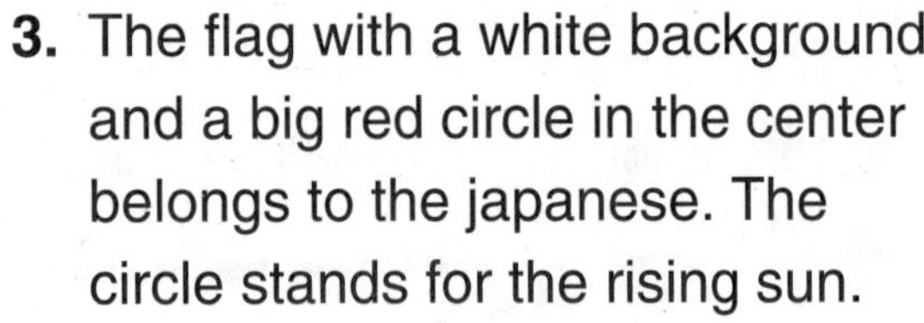

3. The flag with a white background and a big red circle in the center belongs to the japanese. The circle stands for the rising sun.

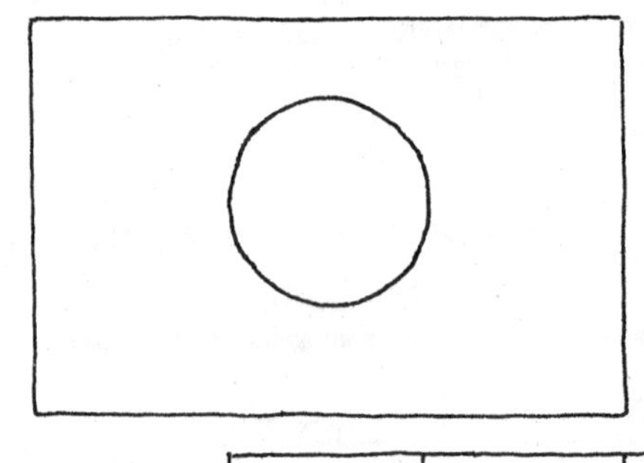

____

4. The french flag is divided lengthwise into three separate bands. From left to right it is blue, white, and red.

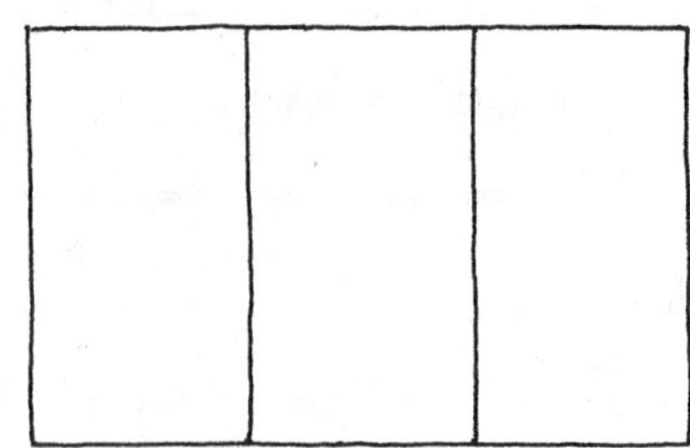

____

5. At the brazilian embassy, you would see this flag with its green background. In the center there is a blue globe on a yellow diamond. The center of the globe has a white line indicating the equator.

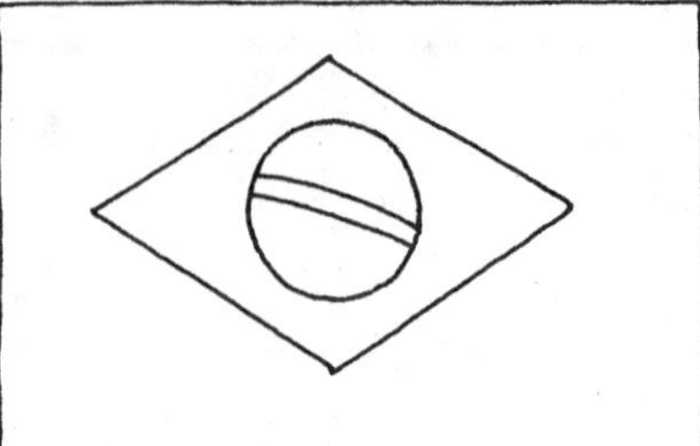

____

At Home: Design your own flag. Then write a description of it using a proper adjective.

Name______________________ Date__________ **Extend 56**

Mixed Review

Read all the sentences in each riddle. Then add the missing articles and adjectives. Finally, answer each riddle.

1. It has ______________ legs.
   It has a pair of wings.
   It has three ______________ parts.
   It may hop, crawl, or fly.
   What is it?
   It's ______________

2. It has scales.
   It crawls on ______________ ground.
   It may be poisonous.
   It is cold-blooded.
   What is it?
   It's ______________

3. It has two wings.
   It has very ______________ skinny legs.
   It is big but does not fly.
   It sometimes puts its head in the sand.
   It's ______________

4. It is orange with ______________ stripes.
   It's ______________ wild mammal that lives in Asia.
   It purrs and growls.
   It's ______________

At Home: Write up a riddle about a famous person, thing, or place to ask a family member. Try to include a proper adjective in your riddle.

▶ **Critical Thinking**

Name____________________ Date__________ **Extend 57**

Adjectives That Compare

Circle the adjective that compares in each sentence. Then, if you can, write the answer to the question on the line.

1. Which Wright brother was older, Wilbur or Orville? __________
2. Which ocean is deeper, the Atlantic or the Pacific? __________
3. True or False: Mount Everest is the highest mountain in the world. __________
4. Which lake is longer, Lake Michigan or Lake Superior? __________
5. Is the Sears Tower in Chicago taller or shorter than the World Trade Center in New York? __________
6. True or False: The world's longest river is the Amazon. __________
7. True or False: Delaware is the smallest state in the U.S.A. __________
8. Is the highest U.S. mountain found in California or Alaska? __________
9. True or False: The cheetah is the fastest land animal. __________
10. True or False: Plains are lower than the land around them. __________
11. True or False: The oldest Moon rock brought back by the Apollo astronauts is about 4.6 billion years old. __________
12. Which planet is closest to the sun? __________
13. Which planet is the largest? __________
14. Which planet is closer to the sun, Earth or Pluto? __________

At Home: Compare five facts about your state with five facts of a neighboring state.

Name ____________________ Date __________ **Extend 58**

Spelling Adjectives That Compare

A. Complete the chart by adding adjectives that compare. Watch the spelling!

Adjective	Compares Two Nouns	Compares Three or More Nouns
big	______	______
brave	______	______
early	______	______
funny	______	______
gloomy	______	______
happy	______	______
hot	______	______
sad	______	______
sorry	______	______
wise	______	______

B. Write five sentences using words from the last two columns of the chart.

____

____

____

____

____

At Home: Write three sentences that compare things in your home. For example: *The mat at the front door is larger than the one at the back door.*

▶ **Critical Thinking**

Name________________________ Date____________ **Extend 59**

Comparing with *More* and *Most*

The Little League playoffs are on! Here are the scoreboards for two different games. Read the questions below and answer each one in a complete sentence, using *more* or *most.*

Inning	1	2	3	4	5	6
Tigers	0	2	1	3	0	3
Lions	2	0	2	5	3	1

Inning	1	2	3	4	5	6
Sharks	4	1	0	3	2	4
Whales	2	1	3	3	2	4

1. Which team had the most impressive first inning?

____

2. Which of the two games was more exciting, and why?

____

____

3. Which team faced the most difficult challenge in the sixth inning, and why?

____

____

4. Which team had a more upsetting loss than the Sharks?

____

At Home: What do you like about baseball? Write a short paragraph. Use *more* and *most* when you can.

Name_______________________________ Date______________ **Extend 60**

Comparing with *Good* and *Bad*

A. Use *good, better,* and *best* in each of the following sentences.

1. On the baseball field, I am ____________________ at catching fly balls, but Jim is ____________________ than I at fielding grounders, and Sarah is the ____________________ catcher ever.

2. In the music room, Jim is the ____________________ trumpet player in his age group, and Sarah is ____________________ than I at the piano; I am simply ____________________ but not great.

3. In art class, Sarah's paintings are ____________________, but mine are ____________________ than hers, and Jim's are ____________________ of all.

4. In science class, Jim's projects are usually ____________________, Sarah's are ____________________ than his and mine are always the ____________________ in the class.

B. Use *bad, worse,* and *worst* in each of the following sentences.

5. I have to admit I am ____________________ at writing letters, and Sarah is ____________________ than I, but the ____________________ letter writer of all is Jim.

6. Jim is also ____________________ at returning phone calls; I'm just a bit ____________________, but Sarah is ____________________ of all three of us.

7. All three of us are ____________________ at cleaning up our cubbies, but I think Sarah is the ____________________ of us three, and mine always looks ____________________ than Jim's.

8. In gym class I am ____________________ on the swings, but Jim is ____________________ than I, and Sarah is ____________________ of all!

At Home: Write about a skill you do well and a skill you want to improve. How will you go about it?

▶ **Critical Thinking**

Name ______________________ Date ____________ **Extend 61**

Combining Sentences: Adjectives

Pretend you wrote the following "draft" as a report for school. Now it's time to improve your writing. Rewrite the paragraph below. Combine sentences by moving an adjective from one sentence to another.

A Day at a Museum

Mom took me to a museum yesterday. It was a natural history museum. We saw many dinosaur skeletons. The skeletons were huge. We saw fossils of footprints. The footprints were enormous. We read signs. The signs were informative. The Mesozoic era includes three periods. They are the Cretaceous, the Jurassic, and the Triassic.

I read about the *Allosaurus. Allosaurus* means "other lizard." It had a big body. It was 35 feet long. It had many teeth. Its teeth were sharp. Of course, it had a big jaw. Its jaw was powerful. It was a meat eater. It had two small forelegs. Each foreleg had three claws. The claws served as meat hooks. The claws were curved.

A Day at a Museum

____

____

____

____

____

____

____

____

____

____

At Home: Create new names for other dinosaurs you know about and describe them in a paragraph.

▶ **Critical Thinking**

Name________________________________ Date______________ **Extend 62**

Mechanics and Usage: Letter Punctuation

Add the correct punctuation and capital letters to Jillian's letter. Then pretend you are Josephine and answer the letter. Use your own address in the letter you write.

october 7 2003

57 east fairware st

Park city, utah 84060

dear josephine

I can't believe it. I read in today's paper that ordinary people will be able to visit the moon soon. I have mixed feelings about going. Traveling in space just has to be a wonderful feeling. But I think I would be lonely for my friends if I stayed away for a long time. I would miss my parents and, yes, even my little brother.

Write to me and tell me what you think.

love jillian

____

____

____

____

____

____

____

____

____

____

____

At Home: Explain the advantages and disadvantages of living in a big city in a letter to a friend. Mail your letter or share it with a family member.

▶ **Critical Thinking**

Name________________________________ Date______________ **Extend 63**

Mixed Review

A. Complete the sentences with the correct comparative adjectives.

1. The blue whale is the ____________________ mammal in the world.

2. An elephant is ____________________ than a whale but ____________________ than a hippopotamus.

3. The ____________________ nose belongs to the African elephant.

4. The ostrich has a ____________________ neck than the flamingo.

5. A tortoise is ____________________ to watch than a slug.

6. The peacock has the ____________________ tail feathers of any other bird.

7. The Egyptian goose is the ____________________ flier of all birds.

8. The ____________________ zoo I have ever seen had small, dirty cages.

9. A zoo with a lot of wide open spaces is ____________________ than one with only tiny cages.

10. One of the ____________________ zoos in the world is in San Diego, California.

B. Underline the proper adjectives in the sentences above.

C. Combine the following sentences by adding an adjective to one sentence.

11. The giant anteater's tail is very long. The giant anteater's tail is sticky.

____

12. The Nile River alligator has a large jaw with many teeth. The Nile River alligator has sharp teeth.

____

At Home: Make up a fact book about people or animals. Use comparative adjectives in your book. Share your work with a family member.

▶ **Critical Thinking**

Name________________________________ Date_____________ **Extend 64**

Common Errors: Adjectives

A. Read the story and underline the incorrect comparative adjectives. Write the correct adjectives on the lines below.

Clara's grandparents run Gardini's, one of the most popularest restaurants in town. It is the most hardest place to get a reservation. Other restaurants are much more fancier. Gardini's is most best for families and for people who like food made with the most freshest ingredients. Clara helps out during the most busiest times. Grandfather is the most nicest person, and he never loses his temper, even when the most worst catastrophes happen in the kitchen! Grandmother is demandinger, but she works in the kitchen and helps wait on tables, too, so her job is hecticer than Grandfather's. Grandfather and Grandmother agree that Clara is the most quickest table-setter there is. Sometimes Grandmother tells her to be more carefuller, but Clara has never broken a dish. When the restaurant is quiet, Clara fixes herself the most biggest bowl of soup and sits down to the most wonderfullest meal anywhere. Her grandparents are importanter to her than anyone else.

1. ________ **6.** ________ **11.** ________

2. ________ **7.** ________ **12.** ________

3. ________ **8.** ________ **13.** ________

4. ________ **9.** ________ **14.** ________

5. ________ **10.** ________ **15.** ________

B. What is your favorite restaurant? Write about the last time your family ate out. Use comparative adjectives to describe your meal.

____

____

____

At Home: Write about your grandparents or another relative. Tell why that person is special to you. Use adjectives that compare.

▶ **Critical Thinking**

Name________________________ Date____________ **Extend 65**

Study Skills: Maps

Bei is studying United States history. She studied this map showing the settlers' original thirteen colonies and the areas settled by 1820 and by 1850.

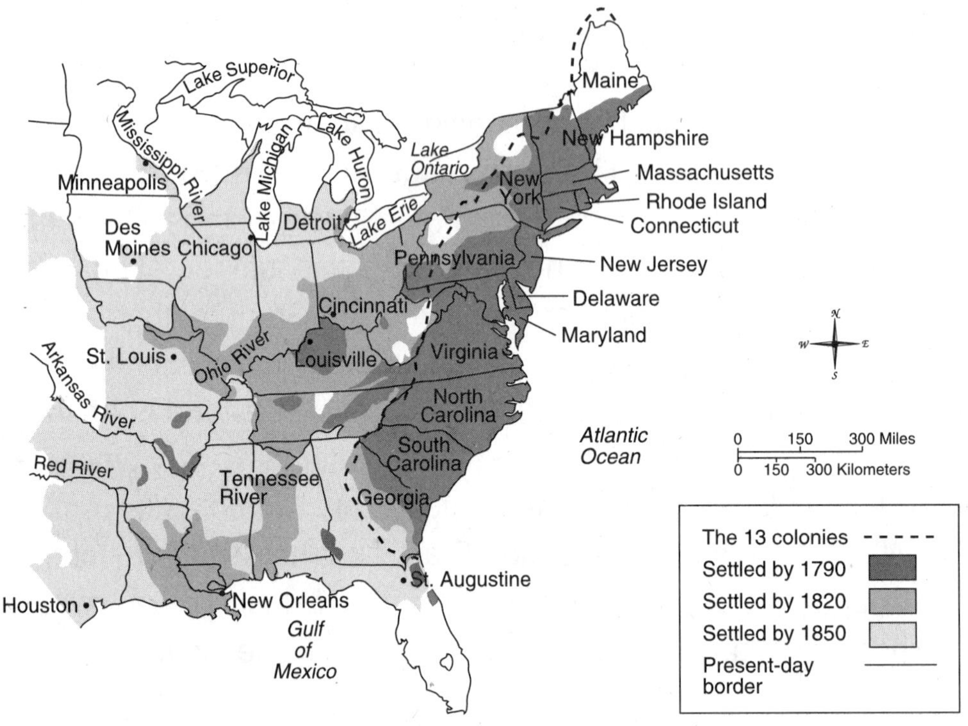

Use the information on the map to complete the sentences below.

1. In 1820, two modern-day cities north of St. Louis that were not yet settled were ____________________ and ____________________.
2. The ____________________ is the body of water to the east of the thirteen colonies.
3. By 1820, the southernmost city that was settled was ____________________.
4. By 1850, the cities of ____________________ and ____________________ were settled. They were as far south as the southernmost settled city in 1820.
5. The ____________________ River had two settled cities on its banks by 1820. By 1850, more land was settled to the west and south of it.

At Home: Make some comparisons between settlements in 1850 and the United States today.

Name ______________________ Date __________ **Extend 66**

Vocabulary: Synonyms and Antonyms

Find a synonym or antonym for each word in the word search puzzle below. Look for words across, down, and diagonally. Circle the word in the puzzle, then write it on the correct line.

Synonyms

neat	______________	recreation	______________
error	______________	ask	______________
glisten	______________	choose	______________

Antonyms

before	______________	worry	______________
beautiful	______________	more	______________
sunrise	______________	ruin	______________

V	U	M	C	B	T	O	F	I
C	D	S	E	R	I	O	U	S
U	T	R	F	R	D	Y	N	E
H	O	M	E	L	Y	T	X	L
D	S	I	M	P	E	A	S	E
U	H	S	N	O	A	S	W	C
S	I	T	X	C	Z	I	S	T
K	N	A	F	T	E	R	R	D
R	E	K	C	A	L	M	B	O
Q	U	E	S	T	I	O	N	N

At Home: Create a crossword puzzle using the above words.

▶ **Critical Thinking**

Name ______________________ Date ____________ **Extend 67**

Composition: Organization

A. Find the time-order words and spatial words in the paragraph below and write them in the chart.

When I first came to Wildwood School, I didn't know anyone. I sat beside a girl named Wendy. Wendy sat next to a boy named Fred. As soon as I sat down, Wendy and Fred asked me my name and where I was from. Then they introduced me to a few more kids in the class. When the teacher came in, she had me stand up in front of the group. I had to give a little speech about myself and then go over to the map and show the class my hometown. Later I went to lunch with Fred and another boy named Carlo. His grandmother lives near the city I used to live in, and he visited her there a long time ago. After lunch we played outside. Wendy and Carlo and I climbed on top of the play structure, and we played wall ball. Ever since that day, Wendy and Carlo and Fred have been my good friends, and I feel lucky that I moved to such a nice place!

Time-order Words	Spatial Words

B. What is it like to be the new kid in a situation? On another sheet of paper, use time-order words and spatial words to tell about how you have made new friends.

At Home: Discuss with a family member how time-order words and spatial words help you to organize your writing.

Name ______________________ Date ____________ Extend 68

Pronouns

Look at the picture. Then add a pronoun that completes each sentence.

1. ________________ is spring because the trees are budding.
2. The girl who is jumping has a bow in ________________ hair.
3. ________________ is a very good jumper!
4. The girls who are turning the rope have ________________ left hands at ________________ sides.
5. ________________ look like they are having a lot of fun.
6. The dog looks like ________________ wants to jump, too.
7. It seems that the boy has ________________ leash.
8. ________________ must have forgotten to put the leash on the dog.
9. "________________ have to take you home now," said the boy.
10. "________________ are going to the vet in just a little while."

At Home: Explain possible mishaps that can occur when a dog is left off its leash.
▶ **Critical Thinking**

Name______________________________ Date____________ **Extend 69**

Subject Pronouns

Circle all the subject pronouns in the following jokes.

I love to tell riddles and jokes. You will like these:

"We serve anything the customer wants," said a restaurant sign. So I went in and ordered roasted rocket ship and fries. The waiter said, "Certainly, sir." He went into the kitchen. He returned looking sad. "I bet you have no rocket ship," said another customer with a smirk.

"It is not that, sir," answered the waiter. "We have no potatoes."

We asked the waiter, "What's on the menu today?"

He answered, "Everything."

I said, "Bring us everything, then."

He shouted to the cook, "Two orders of hash!"

She asked the waiter, "Will the pancakes be long?"

"No, Madam, they will be round, as usual."

At Home: Create a menu for a silly restaurant. Describe each item. Circle any subject pronouns on your menu.

Name________________________________ Date______________ **Extend 70**

Object Pronouns

Underline the object pronoun in each sentence.

At the Nature Center

Come with me to the wildlife preserve. I will introduce you to Mrs. Whitcomb. She will explain to us how beavers build their ponds. We will be able to see them busy at work.

Mrs. Whitcomb brought along her teenage son, Derek, who helps her. He said he'd take us on a nature walk. I showed him my gold bird feather. He liked it and said we'd look for a bird that had gold feathers.

We saw chipmunk holes and saw two critters scurry down into them. We heard a rat-a-tat-tat, rat-a-tat-tat not too far from us.

"Derek," I asked pointing to a woodpecker up in a tree, "Did my feather come from it?"

"Yes," said Derek, "it looks like a yellow-shafted flicker to me."

At Home: Describe a bird that lives in your neighborhood. Use object pronouns. Then draw a picture of it. Show your work to a family member.

▶ **Critical Thinking**

Name______________________________ Date____________ **Extend 71**

Mechanics and Usage: Punctuation in Dialogue

Pretend you interviewed people for a newspaper story. Below are your notes. Rewrite them as a story for your school paper. Add paragraphs, quotation marks, and other punctuation where needed.

I asked students what they thought of the new after-school program. Jill said I like it because I finish my paintings in the art room. I don't like it said Ali. My parents insist I come, but I would rather play ball with my friends in the park. June said I like it because my mom can't pick me up until 6:00. Later I went to speak to Ms. Freemont who runs the program. She said I think this program has been needed for a long time. I also spoke to Mr. Quimbley, our principal. He said we are lucky that the mayor has given us money for the program. It's going to be the best in the city.

____

____

____

____

____

____

____

____

____

____

At Home: Discuss a current event with a parent. Express your views about it.

Name________________________________ Date______________ **Extend 72**

Mixed Review

A. On the line, write *subject* if the underlined pronoun is a subject pronoun. Write *object* if it is an object pronoun.

1. I like to read folk tales and trickster tales. ______________________
2. They are fun to read aloud. ______________________
3. My younger sister likes me to read them to her. ______________________
4. Then she retells them to me in her own words. ______________________
5. Sometimes my Dad reads trickster tales to both of us. ______________________

B. Underline only the subject and object pronouns in the following tale. Add a title and an ending to the story. Use more subject and object pronouns.

____

One day a small terrier named Spot stole a large steak from a woman's shopping bag. She chased him, but she couldn't catch him. Spot ran with the steak into the woods. On his way, he came to a stream. He looked into the water and saw a dog with a steak in his mouth. Spot jumped into the water to grab the steak from him. And while jumping, he also gave out a loud bark.

Spot no longer saw the other dog or his steak. Spot hungrily watched as the steak was carried away with the current.

____

____

____

____

____

At Home: Write a simple fable or tale. Use subject and object pronouns. Share your tale with a family member.

▶ **Critical Thinking**

Name ______________________ Date __________ **Extend 73**

Pronoun-Verb Agreement

Choose a verb from the word box to complete each sentence. Write the correct form of the verb. Then write the name of the person or thing that the subject pronoun refers to.

eat	feed	fight	go	live	list
reach	speed	spin	vote	wear	write

1. She ______________ fires. ______________
2. It ______________ to a burning building. ______________
3. Together they ______________ the flames. ______________
4. They ______________ the leaves of trees with their long necks. ______________
5. It ______________ a chrysalis and changes into an insect that flies. ______________
6. He ______________ and cares for the gorillas. ______________
7. He ______________ in the White House. ______________
8. They ______________ laws for our country. ______________
9. We ______________ for our lawmakers. ______________
10. We ______________ there when we don't want to stay home and cook. ______________
11. He ______________ a hat when he prepares food. ______________
12. It ______________ the specials of the day. ______________

At Home: Create five more sentences like those above. Read them to family members and ask who or what the subject refers to.

▶ **Critical Thinking**

Name_______________________________ Date_____________ **Extend 74**

Combining Sentences

Combine the sentences by joining two or more pronouns in the subject or the predicate. You may want to replace two singular pronouns with a plural pronoun.

1. You have a book on volcanoes. He has a book on volcanoes.

____

2. I will place the books on the shelf. She will place the books on the shelf.

____

3. He works the computer. You work the computer.

____

4. She helped her get on-line. I helped her get on-line.

____

5. Sophie thanked me. Sophie thanked her.

____

6. Mrs. Reasoner said he and she talk too much. Mrs. Reasoner said I talk too much, too.

____

7. You can find pictures in that file next to him. You can find pictures in that file next to me.

____

8. Phillipa dropped a stack of books near him. I dropped a stack of books near her.

____

9. "Too much noise," she said. "Too much noise," he said.

____

10. Will you walk her home? Will you walk me home?

____

At Home: Discuss ideas for a neighborhood book swap.

▶ **Critical Thinking**

Name____________________ Date__________ **Extend 75**

Possessive Pronouns

Complete the sentences by adding possessive pronouns.

________________ parents are planning a family vacation. Mom wants to visit ________________ mother in Seattle. Dad wants to use ________________ new camping gear somewhere in the mountains. ________________ sister and I told them we wanted to stay home and play with ________________ new friends who just moved in across the street. ________________ new puppy is adorable, and we all like to play with it. Its ears flop around ________________ eyes. We were just kidding, but ________________ parents, didn't realize it.

"Why can't we make everyone happy?" ________________ father asked Mom. "You can visit ________________ mother. Then you and I will go camping with ________________ new gear, and the kids can stay home with a babysitter."

"________________ idea is not a good one," I said.

"We have changed ________________ minds," said ________________ sister.

"Oh," said Dad, "I bet you want to go to ________________ favorite amusement park."

"________________ hunch is right," I said. "We really want to visit Grandmother, go camping with you, and go to an amusement park, too."

"That settles that," said Dad. "Now everyone is happy."

At Home: Write about a vacation you would enjoy with your family. Use possessive pronouns.

Name________________________________ Date____________ **Extend 76**

Mechanics and Usage: Contractions, Pronouns and Verbs

Enjoy the jokes. Then change a pronoun and a verb to a contraction to make the writing smoother.

Teacher: Peter, name two pronouns.

Peter: Who, me?

Teacher: You are right! ____________________

Tim: If I gave you three gerbils this afternoon and three tomorrow, how many would you have?

Peter: Eight. I have got two already. ____________________

Dad: Peter, you have got your shoes on the wrong feet. ____________________

Peter: They are the only feet I have. ____________________

Teacher: Get out your chemistry book. We are going to study nitrates. Peter, tell us what you know about nitrates. ____________________

Peter: Mom says they are usually twice the day rates. ____________________

Mom: Peter, I wish you would pay a little more attention. ____________________

Peter: I am paying as little attention as possible. ____________________

Peter: I have just had a brilliant idea. ____________________

Lee: It is probably beginner's luck. ____________________

At Home: Write a joke or riddle about a child and a parent. Share it with a family member.

▶ **Critical Thinking**

Name ______________________ Date ____________ **Extend 77**

Mixed Review

A. Add a present, past, or future-tense verb to each sentence as indicated in the parentheses. Make sure the verb agrees with the subject pronoun.

1. He (present) ______________ to make the masks for our school play.
2. She (past) ______________ the last of the script writing.
3. They (future) ______________ on the scenery tomorrow.
4. It (past) ______________ to the ground yesterday.
5. We all (past) ______________ it up and made it stand again.

B. Combine the following sentences.

6. Are you in the play? Is he in the play?

____

7. I asked him to be a talking tree. I asked her to be a talking tree.

____

8. He turned down the part. She turned down the part.

____

9. She said she wanted to work the lights. He said he wanted to work the lights.

____

10. They were getting frustrated. I was getting frustrated.

____

C. Write a sentence that includes the possessive pronoun in parentheses. Will you use it in the subject or the predicate? Try to stick with the "class play" theme.

11. (my) ______________________________
12. (your) ______________________________

At Home: Write some dialogue for a skit. Use subject, object, and possessive pronouns. Read your dialogue out loud with a family member. Each of you read a part.

▶ **Critical Thinking**

Name____________________ Date__________ **Extend 78**

Common Errors: Pronouns

Marcy made the following speech at the school assembly, telling about an honor that she and her classmates received. Choose the correct pronouns and write them on the lines to finish the sentences in the speech.

The students in Mrs. Rey's class are happy to announce that ____________ have been chosen to represent Hill School at the City Art Show. The show will be held the third weekend in April, and ____________ purpose is to raise money for the people of Carter County. As ____________ know, many of ____________ lost their homes in the recent flood. ____________ want to do everything ____________ can to help. The mural that ____________ class designed will be hanging in the lobby at City Hall. The mural is over 12 feet long, and ____________ shows the city skyline. The mayor, who was one of the judges, said ____________ had never seen such a wonderful collage. ____________ used a variety of things to create ____________ masterpiece. ____________ is very colorful and busy, and ____________ will see that lots of familiar city sights have been included in the scene. Mrs. Andrews said that ____________ will take a group to the show on Saturday morning. ____________ urge ____________ to try and come along. ____________ will be a fun trip, and ____________ is for a good cause. If ____________ have any questions, don't hesitate to contact ____________ or someone else in Mrs. Rey's class.

At Home: What kind of money-raising projects are going on in your community? Write up an announcement for a cause that interests you. Be sure to use pronouns correctly.

▶ **Critical Thinking**

Name________________________ Date__________ **Extend 79**

Study Skills: Dictionary

Tori read an editorial in her school newspaper. She was unsure of the meanings of some of the words, so she used information from the dictionary to create her own personal dictionary.

Use Tori's personal dictionary and write the part of speech and meaning for each underlined word in the editorial.

A perfect complement to a school day is a late afternoon full of fun activities. It is a principal concern of teachers and parents that students find clubs or teams they can enjoy. Some students believe it is a capital idea to join a club, like the drama club. Others choose another course of action—that is, a sports team. Teachers are happy to counsel students about their choices. We encourage everyone to try out some new activities but not desert their favorites.

1. complement ______________________
2. principal ______________________
3. capital ______________________
4. course ______________________
5. counsel ______________________
6. desert ______________________

capital (kap´ i təl) *adj.* **1.** most important **2.** where government is located **3.** excellent; very fine **4.** that which is punished by death *n.* **1.** upper case letter **2.** place where government is located **3.** money or property **4.** the top part of a column

complement (kom´ plə mənt) *n.* **1.** something that completes or makes perfect **2.** the full number needed **3.** the word(s) that complete a predicate *v.* to make complete or perfect by supplying what is needed.

counsel (koun´ səl) *n.* **1.** advice or opinion **2.** exchanging ideas by talking together **3.** lawyer(s) who handle a case *v.* **1.** to give advice **2.** to urge or recommend

course (kôrs) *n.* **1.** path of action **2.** a choice that continues over time **3.** a direction taken **4.** a way of acting **5.** like things in an order **6.** part of a meal **7.** a single or complete series of studies in a subject *v.* to run or race through

desert (di zûrt´) *v.* **1.** to leave **2.** to abandon a military position or post without permission *n.* (de´ zûrt) **1.** a dry, sandy region **2.** wild and not lived in

principal (prin´ sə pəl) *adj.* **1.** most important *n.* **1.** a person or thing of first importance **2.** the head of a school **3.** sum of money invested or owed, not counting interest.

At Home: Select a word from the editorial and a meaning other than the one used in the editorial. Write a sentence showing how it is used.

▶ **Critical Thinking**

Name________________________ Date____________ **Extend 80**

Vocabulary: Homophones and Homographs

Complete the puzzle by writing the correct homophone or homograph.

Across

1. Part of a tree

3. Past tense of *eat*

5. A ______________ of shoes

6. A peck on the cheek

8. It cost 5 ______________.

10. When you cry, ______________ flow from your eyes.

11. "When the ______________ blows, the cradle will rock."

Down

1. If you ______________ a vase, it will shatter into many pieces.

2. A kind of rabbit

4. It follows seven.

7. Part of a play

9. You go up and down these.

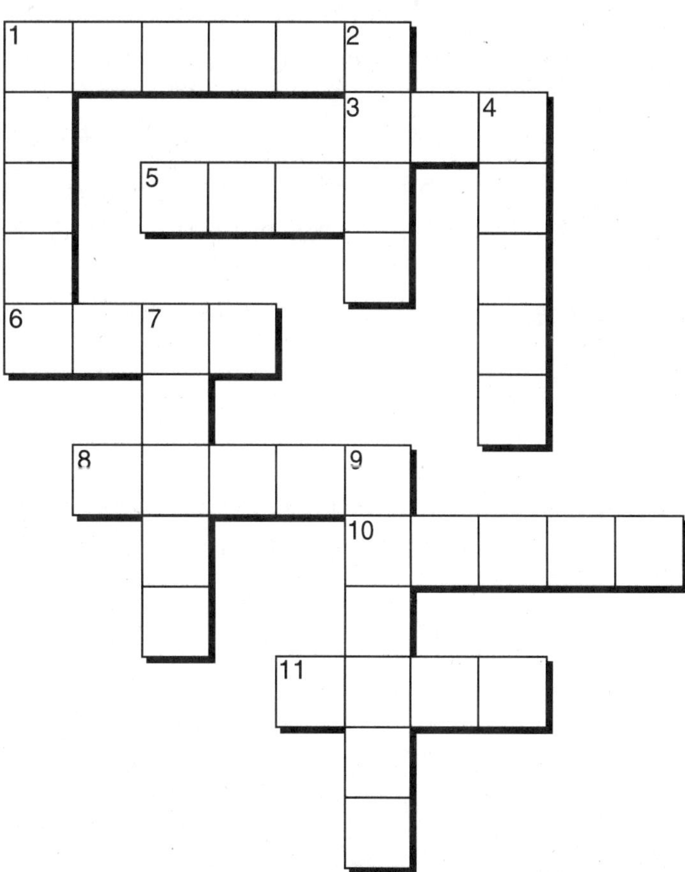

At Home: Use the answers from the puzzle to write a few pairs of homophones. For example, a homophone pair for 2 Down is *hair-hare.*

▶ **Critical Thinking**

Name________________________ Date____________ **Extend 81**

Composition: Writing Dialogue

Read the dialogue examples below. Then answer the questions.

"I told Ed that the bus would be late," said Bill, "so he got a ride with Jess."

1. Who is the speaker? ____________________

"Glen is in my class," said Hattie. "He seems nice." "He is nice," said Lisa. "I sat with him last year."

2. Who is having this dialogue? ____________________

3. What should be done to correct this dialogue?

____

"Do you have a new bike, Kim? asked Lucy. "No, I just cleaned up my old one!" said Kim.

4. Who is asking the question? ____________________

5. What should be done to correct this dialogue?

____

"Do you have the homework assignment?" asked Bruno. "I don't have it, said Ben, but I think Carly does."

6. Name the person Bruno is talking to. ____________________

7. What should be done to correct this dialogue?

____

"could you pick up a quart of milk for me?" asked Mom. "Sure," said Tom. "I'll bring it home after school.

8. Name the person Tom is talking to. ____________________

9. What should be done to correct this dialogue?

____

____

At Home: Whom do you like to talk to? Call a friend, and then jot down your conversation. Be sure to punctuate your dialogue correctly.

Name________________________________ Date______________ **Extend 82**

Adverbs That Tell *How*

A. Underline the adverb in each tongue twister. Then circle the verb that the adverb describes.

1. Fred frantically flees fifty-five flying fireflies.
2. Peter Piper prudently picked pitted plums.
3. Wally Williams wildly whacks whiffle balls.
4. Speedily, Suzie Smith sprints.
5. Dennis digs diligently in the dusty den.
6. Presley picked a pound of prickly pears perfectly.
7. Señor Sanchez swiftly sheared sixty-seven sheep.
8. Sandy's son suddenly shines several scuffed shoes.
9. Theo fearlessly threw three free throws.
10. Sarah sees the setting sun sink swiftly.

B. Make up two tongue twisters that include adverbs.

11. ____

____

12. ____

____

At Home: Take the challenge. Write one silly sentence with as many adverbs in it as you can.

▶ **Critical Thinking**

Name________________________________ Date_______________ **Extend 83**

Adverbs That Tell *When* or *Where*

A man sitting on a sidewalk bench on Main Street saw an accident happen in the middle of the street. A police officer asked him to write a report of what he saw. Here is what he wrote.

Underline all the adverbs that tell where or when. Then write them on the lines below.

The accident happened today right here in the middle of Main Street. I was outside waiting for a friend. I was early. The accident happened suddenly on Main Street. The taxi was parked near the curb. It quickly pulled out and rammed the convertible's back right fender. The woman stood in front of her convertible and called 911 on her cell phone. Then she drove her car to the side of the road. The taxi driver remained in his taxi. Finally, the police arrived.

_______________ _______________ _______________ _______________

_______________ _______________ _______________ _______________

_______________ _______________

At Home: Write detailed directions on how to get from your home to a relative's house.

Name____________________ Date__________ **Extend 84**

Adverbs That Compare

Add *-er* or *-est* to each adverb in parentheses. Write the word on the line to make the sentence read correctly.

My Puppy

It's been (hard) ____________________ to convince my mom than my dad to get me a puppy. Mom first said that the (early) __________________ I can get one is next spring. That was (long) ____________________ than I had expected to wait. I promised to walk, feed, and brush the dog every day.

Finally, Mom answered in her (strong) ____________________ voice ever, "Okay, I give in. You'll get your puppy (soon) ____________________ than next spring."

Dad said that we could visit an animal shelter that is (near)__________________ to his office than to my Mom's. The (early) __________________ Dad said he could take me was next Saturday. The (close) __________________ Saturday came, the more excited I got.

I now have the cutest puppy you can imagine. It barks (loud) ____________________ in the evening than it does in the daytime. It jumps (high) ____________________ than my knees. Best of all, it sleeps and snores softly in my room every night.

At Home: What kind of pet would you suggest to a friend? Write instructions for someone on how to care for that pet.

▶ **Critical Thinking**

Name____________________________________ Date________________ **Extend 85**

More Adverbs That Compare

Add *more* or *most* to complete each sentence.

1. Jody waited the ____________________ anxiously of anyone in class.
2. Troy learned his lines ____________________ slowly than Phil.
3. Jody recited her lines ____________________ eloquently of all.
4. The scene that takes place in Bali passed the ____________________ swiftly of all the scenes.
5. The males danced ____________________ rhythmically than the females.
6. We rehearsed ____________________ determinedly today than yesterday.
7. Ramon painted ____________________ frantically than Jordon to finish the scenery on time.
8. He drew the trees ____________________ quickly than he did the bushes.
9. Our auditorium can seat guests ____________________ comfortably than our cafeteria.
10. My parents cheer and applaud ____________________ loudly of all the parents.

At Home: Use *more* and *most* to compare the outdoor activities that you and your family engage in.

Mechanics and Usage: *Good* and *Well*

Add *good* or *well* to complete each sentence.

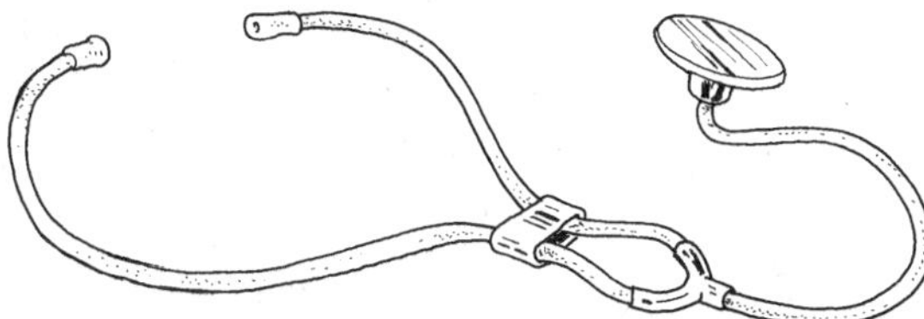

"It's always a ____________________ idea to maintain ____________________ health habits," said Ms. Taylor, our school nurse. "If you want to keep healthy and ____________________, you have to eat good foods. You also must do a ____________________ amount of physical exercise every day."

"Who can demonstrate some ____________________ exercises?" she asked.

Belinda offered to show us how to do push-ups. She did them quite ____________________. Ms. Taylor said, "____________________ job, Belinda!"

Then Ms. Taylor asked us to list ____________________ healthful foods that are part of the food pyramid. Anna writes ____________________, so she listed the foods on the chalkboard, and we copied them in our notebooks.

Then it was time to be weighed and measured, so we went to Ms. Taylor's office. "You have gained only a pound since the fall, and that's ____________________ for your height," Ms. Taylor told Amy.

"Oh, dear, you don't look ____________________," said Ms. Taylor, looking at Joseph's eyes. She checked his forehead to see if he had a fever. "I think it would be ____________________ if you went home now. I am sure you will get ____________________

At Home: Make a poster that shows how to keep safe in your home. Show it to a family member.

▶ Critical Thinking

Name ______________________ Date ____________ **Extend 87**

Mixed Review

A. Underline the adverb in each sentence. Then on the line, write *how, where,* or *when* to tell what question the adverb answers.

1. He ran quietly through the house. ______________________
2. He ran up against the tabby yesterday. ______________________
3. That feline was extremely fast. ______________________
4. He stayed close to the entrance. ______________________
5. He knew that cat stayed around. ______________________

B. Write an adverb that compares the actions.

6. This frog leaped ______________ than the one over there.
7. Grandma screamed the ______________ when one frog jumped into the punch bowl.
8. We kids scurried ______________ than the grownups, as we tried to catch them.
9. The dog barked ______________ than I had ever heard him bark before.
10. We all laughed ______________ than ever before!

C. Create a crossword puzzle or a word search puzzle which includes adverbs on this page. Run off copies of your puzzle and share it with classmates.

At Home: Use *good* and *well* in two separate sentences. Share your sentences with family members.

Name______________________ Date__________ **Extend 88**

Negatives

Baby Talk

Sometimes when learning to talk, toddlers use more than one negative in a sentence. Rewrite each of the following sentences so that each one has only one negative word.

1. I don't never want to go to bed.

   ____

2. Nobody never plays with me.

   ____

3. I can't find my socks nowhere.

   ____

4. I haven't no more cookies.

   ____

5. You aren't never going to find me!

   ____

6. I didn't do nothing!

   ____

7. She doesn't like me no more.

   ____

8. No one can find my puzzle pieces nowhere.

   ____

9. They can't do none of it.

   ____

10. I'm not no baby; I'm a big boy.

   ____

At Home: Write a paragraph about something humorous a young child might say or do. Check the paragraph for two negatives in one sentence.

▶ **Critical Thinking**

Name____________________ Date__________ **Extend 89**

Prepositions

Unscramble the sentences and write them on the lines. Then underline the preposition in each sentence. Three lines from well-known nursery rhymes are included. Find and circle them.

Scrambled Sentences

1. fence cat is the on the

2. the treetop bird flew to the

3. puppy ran under porch the the

4. the clock ran mouse up the

5. vegetable the garden far is tree from the apple

6. an old lived shoe there who was woman in a

7. behind is the tree Jorge

8. cat the climb Jorge up tree the and

9. dish away with spoon the ran the

10. toward tree Paula running is the

At Home: What was your favorite nursery rhyme when you were younger? Write it and circle any prepositions you find.

▶ **Critical Thinking**

Name________________________________ Date______________ **Extend 90**

Prepositional Phrases

Read each story starter and underline the prepositional phrase in each one. Then write one sentence that will continue each story.

1. There was an old rabbit beneath an old oak tree.

   ____

2. Beyond the bridge three dragons protected the castle.

   ____

3. The young boy lost his way in the deep dark woods.

   ____

4. Out popped a young dinosaur from the picnic basket.

   ____

5. It was green from top to bottom.

   ____

6. The police were on patrol all night long.

   ____

7. The telephone was ringing off the hook.

   ____

8. Grandma told me this story while sitting on her porch swing.

   ____

9. The bear was right between us!

   ____

10. I jumped right into the swimming hole.

   ____

At Home: Choose a story from above to complete. Write it or tell it to a family member.

▶ **Critical Thinking**

Name________________________________ Date______________ **Extend 91**

Combining Sentences: Complex Sentences

Use the conjunctions in the word box to combine each pair of sentences.

although	because	while	since	when	yet

1. I was digging in our backyard. I found an arrowhead.

____

____

2. I asked my dad a lot of questions. He told me what he knew.

____

____

3. Uncovering objects takes a long time. Archaeologists do not want to harm any treasures.

____

____

4. Archaeologists have helped us learn about the past. There is still a lot more to learn.

____

____

5. Scientists want to know how old an object is. They test the carbon in an object.

____

____

6. Some pictures are painted on cave walls. Others are painted on rocks.

____

____

At Home: Explain the difference between an *archaeologist* and a *paleontologist.* Use conjunctions to combine some sentences in your explanation.

▶ **Critical Thinking**

Name_________________________ Date______________ **Extend 92**

Mechanics and Usage: Commas

Add commas where they belong. Read the skit aloud with a partner. Pause after a comma.

Jody: Liz why didn't you come to chorus practice?

Liz: Well Samantha don't you remember I had my art class after school?

Jody: No I forgot.

Liz: Mr. Lennard said I could miss one practice a week Jody.

Jody: Yes I remember now. That's because you always sing on key.

Liz: No that's not really true, but I do learn the lyrics fast.

Jody: Well I wish I could say the same.

Liz: You won't believe this but Mr. Lennard said I wasn't ready to sing that solo.

Jody: No really? I'll help you practice Liz.

Liz: What a friend you are, Jody!

Jody: Liz would you like to help me out?

Liz: Sure Jody just name it.

Jody: Grab a spoon friend and help me finish this banana split!

At Home: Add a narrator's part to the beginning and ending of the skit above. Use commas in the dialogue.

▶ **Critical Thinking**

Name_______________________ Date___________ **Extend 93**

Mixed Review

A. First, rewrite each sentence to correct the double negative. Then underline the prepositions in the sentences.

1. I never see no one I know at the movie theater.

____

2. If I call from here, she won't never believe me.

____

3. Nobody never told me it was about a scary monster.

____

4. Since the robot couldn't never help, I jumped under my seat.

____

B. Create complex sentences with the pairs of sentences. Then underline the prepositional phrases in each complex sentence.

5. On Wednesdays, I go to a pottery class. I work on the potter's wheel.

____

____

6. I made a bowl for my mother. She likes what I make.

____

7. My teacher wants to exhibit the bowl in a show. She likes it very much.

____

____

8. I will start on a vase. I am finished glazing the bowl.

____

At Home: Write a letter to a friend. Use at least three complex sentences. Ask a family member to proof your letter before you mail it.

▶ **Critical Thinking**

Name________________________________ Date______________ **Extend 94**

Common Errors: Adverbs

A. Read the fable below. Correct any errors you find in how adverbs and double negatives have been used. Make corrections above the lines.

The Fox and the Grapes

Once upon a time there was a fox who could not never get enough grapes. Every day, he looked careful and sniffed the air deep to find grapes to eat. One day he stopped sudden in his tracks. Dangling inviting above his head was the most beautiful cluster of grapes he had ever seen!

"Oh boy!" he said excited. "I can't not wait to taste those grapes."

The fox stretched on his tiptoes until he thought he would complete come apart, but he couldn't not reach the grapes. He ran swift and leaped graceful into the air, but he still couldn't not reach the grapes.

"This is not good," he muttered angry. "I will not never taste those grapes."

The fox stubborn kept jumping and leaping and reaching. After trying over and over to snag those grapes, he was final forced to give up.

"I didn't never really want to eat those grapes anyway," he said. "I'm sure they were sour."

B. On a separate sheet of paper, write another ending for this fable. Use adverbs.

At Home: What myths, legends, fables, or fairy tales do you like? Rewrite a traditional story and share it with your family. Be sure to use adverbs correctly.

▶ **Critical Thinking**

Name________________________________ Date______________ **Extend 95**

Study Skills: Encyclopedia

A. Elise and Adam are partners in a research contest. They must look up answers to questions to earn points that will win them first place.

Help them by circling the key word in each question. In which volume of the encyclopedia should they look to find the answers to the questions? Write the volume number in the box to the right of each question.

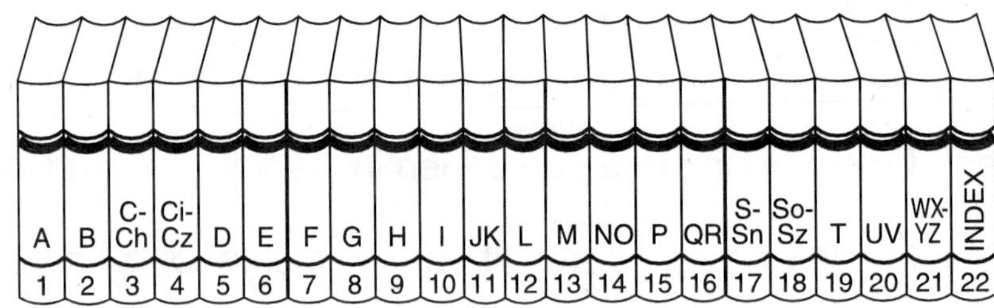

1. When did the painter Maurice Utrillo live? ☐
2. What is the climate of the country of Costa Rica? ☐
3. Who is Maya Angelou? ☐
4. Where is Canterbury located? ☐
5. Who was the father of King Frederick IV of Denmark and Norway? ☐
6. What do you find on the periodic table? ☐
7. Bactra was an ancient Greek kingdom. In what present-day country was Bactra located? ☐
8. What was Isamu Noguchi famous for? ☐
9. What are some traditions of the Hopi people? ☐

B. Write the volume numbers for the questions in the magic square to the right. If your answers are correct, the sum of all the rows, across and down, will be the same.

1	2	3
4	5	6
7	8	9

____

At Home: Make up a question that you can answer by looking up an entry in each volume of the encyclopedia.

Name____________________________ Date____________ **Extend 96**

Vocabulary: Suffixes

Below are definitions. Write the word that is being defined. Remember to add the correct suffix to each word.

1. ________________________: capable of being washed
2. ________________________: without pain
3. ________________________: one who farms
4. ________________________: having dirt
5. ________________________: full of joy
6. ________________________: in misery, capable of being miserable
7. ________________________: in a slow manner
8. ________________________: full of harm
9. ________________________: without thought
10. ________________________: in a complete manner
11. ________________________: result of being excited
12. ________________________: one who mines
13. ________________________: without a brain
14. ________________________: capable of believing
15. ________________________: one who shops

At Home: Include five words from above in a paragraph about someone's occupation.

▶ **Critical Thinking**

Name ______________________ Date ____________ **Extend 97**

Composition: Outlining

Use the words and phrases to fill in an outline for a report about your skeleton. Use the encyclopedia if you need help.

Your skeleton from head to toe		allows for different types of movement		
29 bones in face, head, jaws		6 bones for hearing		
26 bones in foot		femur and ulna		Arms and legs
protects organs		supports your body		opposable thumb
ribcage	Torso	vertebrae	hipbones	Skull

I. ______________________

A. ______________________

B. ______________________

C. ______________________

II. ______________________

A. ______________________

B. ______________________

III. ______________________

A. ______________________

B. ______________________

C. ______________________

IV. ______________________

A. ______________________

B. ______________________

C. ______________________

At Home: How can an outline help you organize your ideas for a report? Use the skeleton outline to write the first paragraph of a report about your bones.

▶ **Critical Thinking**

Name________________ Date________ **Extend 1**

Sentences

Read the posters. Change each fragment to a complete sentence. Then use complete sentences to rewrite the posters in the blank boxes.

Bright Teeth
Perfect Smile
You need:
Glow-White
Toothpaste.
Free toothbrush
with
first purchase

Enter the Art Contest.
Everyone Welcome!
Entry forms must be in by April 8, 2006.
All drawings, paintings, collages accepted.
Prizes!

Possible responses are:
Would you like bright teeth?
You can have bright teeth.
You can have a perfect smile.
A free toothbrush comes with your first purchase.

Possible responses are:
Everyone is welcome.
All drawings, paintings, collages will be accepted.
Prizes will be given.

At Home: Why are sentence fragments effective in posters and some kinds of advertisements? Explain.

▶ **Critical Thinking**

Name________________ Date________ **Extend 2**

Declarative and Interrogative Sentences

The following sentences are either questions or answers for a trivia game. Next to each, write **D** if it is a declarative sentence or **I** if it is an interrogative sentence. Rewrite each sentence and punctuate it correctly. Then draw lines to match each question and answer.

I		II	
1. it is Montpelier	D	**a.** it is known for dairy products	D
It is Montpelier.		It is known for dairy products.	
2. Florida is a peninsula	D	**b.** what is the capital of Vermont	I
Florida is a peninsula.		What is the capital of Vermont?	
3. where do penguins live	I	**c.** what is the 50th state	I
Where do penguins live?		What is the 50th state?	
4. it's a group of islands called Hawaii	D	**d.** what kind of landform is Florida	I
It's a group of islands called Hawaii.		What kind of landform is Florida?	
5. what is Wisconsin known for	I	**e.** it was Betsy Ross	D
What is Wisconsin known for?		It was Betsy Ross.	
6. who designed the first U.S. flag	I	**f.** they live in Antarctica	D
Who designed the first U.S. flag?		They live in Antarctica.	

At Home: Add five more interrogative and declarative sentences to this game.

▶ **Critical Thinking**

Name________________________ Date____________ **Extend 3**

Imperative and Exclamatory Sentences

Three types of sentences are included below. Draw one line under each imperative sentence. Draw two lines under each exclamatory sentence. Then write the sentences in paragraph form. Remember to use correct punctuation.

1. I can hardly believe it
2. I am learning to play tennis
3. Just watch me hit the ball
4. Oh, how hard my teacher makes me work
5. She makes me jog around the court to keep fit
6. No way can I jog around it 5 times
7. Then we volley back and forth
8. Wait until you see how much I have improved
9. Hit a ball to me and you will see
10. Tennis is a terrific game

I can hardly believe it! I am learning to play tennis. Just watch me hit that ball. Oh, how hard my teacher makes me work! She makes me jog around the court to keep fit. No way can I jog around it five times! Then we volley back and forth. Wait until you see how much I have improved. Hit a ball to me and you will see. Tennis is a terrific game!

At Home: What do you know how to do? Write a paragraph titled "How to make a pizza" or "How I learned to play..." Include both exclamatory and imperative sentences.

▶ **Critical Thinking**

Name________________________ Date____________ **Extend 4**

Combining Sentences: Compound Sentences

A. Combine the following pairs of sentences using *and, or,* or *but.* Write each new sentence on the lines.

1. Listen to my riddle.
   Tell me the answer.
   Listen to my riddle, and tell me the answer.
2. This coat has no sleeves.
   It has no buttons.
   This coat has no sleeves, and it has no buttons.
3. It has no pockets.
   It won't keep you warm.
   It has no pockets, and it won't keep you warm.
4. Do you know the answer?
   Can you make a guess?
   Do you know the answer or can you make a guess?
5. I bet you know.
   I'll tell you anyway.
   I bet you know, but I'll tell you anyway.

B. Write your answer to the riddle.

a coat of paint

At Home: Combine the following sentences to include in a cartoon strip. "It is dark inside. I will not go in." Write the sentence in a speech bubble. Add three more frames to the strip.

▶ **Critical Thinking**

Name ____________ Date ________ **Extend 5**

Mechanics and Usage: Sentence Punctuation

Read the letter. Ask yourself if each sentence is declarative, interrogative, imperative, or exclamatory. Then rewrite the paragraph on the lines below. Add the correct punctuation.

Dear Rosa,

what a great Saturday I had listen to this

my parents took me on a nature hike on the trail we saw a chipmunk and we saw some weird-looking birds' nests I wanted to get a close look at a turtle in the brook you won't believe this I fell into the brook and I got my shoes and clothes all wet that water was so cold I began to shiver mom and dad gave me their sweaters Just then, a long green snake slithered from under the log have you ever seen one I was scared and I ran right into the arms of my dad we all had a good laugh I can't wait to go on a nature hike again Come with us next time.

Your pen pal,
Yolanda

Dear Rosa,

What a great Saturday I had! Listen to this.

My parents took me on a nature hike. On the trail we saw a chipmunk, and we saw some weird-looking birds' nests. I wanted to get a close look at a turtle in the brook. You won't believe this! I fell into the brook, and I got my shoes and clothes all wet! That water was so cold! I began to shiver. Mom and Dad gave me their sweaters. Just then, a long green snake slithered from under the log. Have you ever seen one? I was scared, and I ran right into the arms of my dad. We all had a good laugh. I can't wait to go on a nature hike again. Come with us next time.

Your pen pal,
Yolanda

At Home: Pretend you are Rosa. Write a letter to Yolanda. What would you tell her? Use different types of sentences. Punctuate your letter correctly.

▶ **Critical Thinking**

Name ____________ Date ________ **Extend 6**

Mixed Review

A. Write an interrogative sentence about each topic listed. Use the correct punctuation. **Answers will vary, but should contain the correct punctuation.**

1. breakfast: ____________
2. transportation to school: ____________
3. today's lunch: ____________
4. after-school sports: ____________
5. homework: ____________

B. Write a declarative sentence about each topic. Punctuate correctly. Make sure that at least two of your sentences are compound.

6. airport: ____________
7. luggage: ____________
8. ticket: ____________
9. flight attendant: ____________
10. destination: ____________

C. Write an imperative or an exclamatory sentence about each topic.

11. lost in a department store: ____________
12. security guard: ____________
13. new shoes: ____________
14. not enough money: ____________
15. new way home: ____________

At Home: Write five compound sentences using *and, but,* or *or* to combine them. Share your work with a family member.

▶ **Critical Thinking**

Name______________________ Date__________ **Extend** 

Complete Subjects and Complete Predicates

Draw one line under the complete subject. Draw two lines under the complete predicate of each sentence.

My uncle Joe loves to fish. He wakes up before the sun rises and climbs into his small rowboat. Uncle Joe rows down the river. He returns home about midday with a bucket of medium-sized fish. (My Aunt Rita will cook them later for dinner.) Uncle Joe takes off for the country store.

My uncle tells his pals at the store that he had a huge fish on his line. He says that the fish got away because a little boy distracted him.

His story is a very fishy tale.

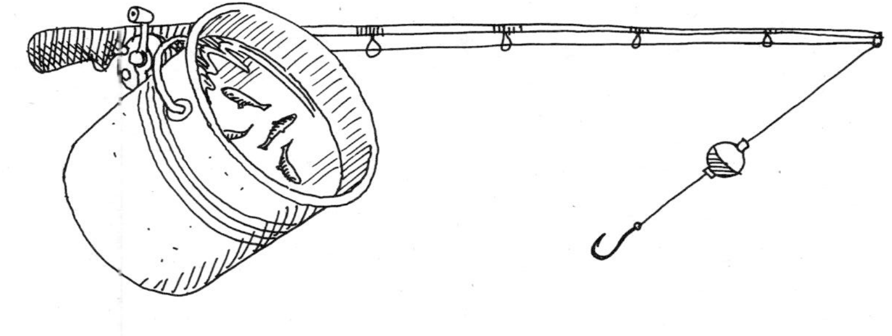

McGraw-Hill Language Arts
Grade 4, Unit 1, Sentences,
pages 14–15

At Home: Think of another reason why Uncle Joe lost his huge fish. Write a paragraph about it.

▶ **Critical Thinking**

Name______________________ Date__________ **Extend 8**

Simple Subjects

Underline the simple subject in each sentence. Then use the simple subject and the crossword clues to fill in the puzzle.

1. Our class is studying the human body. (8 Across)
2. The human body is a great machine. (2 Across)
3. The brain works like a switchboard. (2 Down)
4. Body signals go to and from the brain. (5 Down)
5. Our five senses help us learn about the world. (3 Down)
6. Vibrations help us to hear different sounds. (9 Across)
7. The inner ear contains three bones. (7 Across)
8. Tomorrow an eye doctor is coming to speak to us. (1 Down)
9. We are going to experiment with optical illusions. (4 Across)
10. Nutrition will be a topic later in the week. (6 Across)

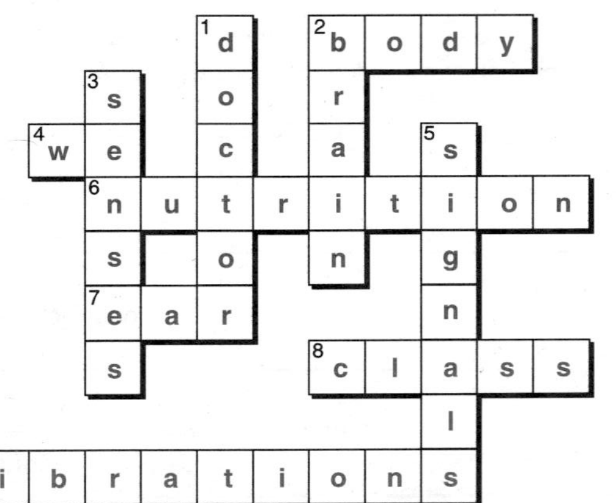

At Home: Design an exercise program that you can put into action three times a week. Write down your goals. Circle the simple subject in each sentence.

▶ **Critical Thinking**

McGraw-Hill Language Arts
Grade 4, Unit 1, Sentences,
pages 16–17

Name_______________ Date_______ **Extend 9**

Simple Predicates

Read the directions below. Underline the simple predicate in each sentence. Then play the game.

1. Play this game with classmates.
2. Print your name on a sheet of paper.
3. Then exchange papers with classmates.
4. Each player writes a silly sentence.
5. Each word of the sentence starts with a letter in the name.
6. What if you get the name "Bud Jones"?
7. Try the following sentence.
8. "Bertha understood David Jackson owed Ned eight sandwiches."
9. Maybe your name is "Robert Jones."
10. "Rod owed Bert eleven round trips just over night every Sunday."

Della
Don't
eat
lavender
lemons
anytime

At Home: Make up a set of directions for your own game using the predicates you underlined above.

▶ **Critical Thinking**

Name_______________ Date_______ **Extend 10**

Combining Sentences: Compound Subjects

Combine each sentence pair by creating a compound subject. Then underline the compound subject in the new sentence.

1. Robert L. Stevenson wrote poetry.
   Shel Silverstein wrote poetry.
   Robert L. Stevenson and Shel Silverstein wrote poetry.

2. Lee-Young read "My Shadow."
   Ruiz read "My Shadow."
   Lee-Young and Ruiz read "My Shadow."

3. Did Shel Silverstein write "Shoe Talk"?
   Did Robert L. Stevenson write "Shoe Talk"?
   Did Shel Silverstein or Robert L. Stevenson write "Shoe Talk"?

4. Limericks are fun to write.
   Haiku poems are fun to write.
   Limericks and haiku poems are fun to write.

5. Sarah will write about Robert L. Stevenson.
   Jamie will write about Robert L. Stevenson.
   Sarah and/or Jamie will write about Robert L. Stevenson.

6. "Mother Doesn't Want a Dog" is my favorite poem.
   "Mother's Nerves" is my favorite poem.
   "Mother Doesn't Want a Dog" and/or "Mother's Nerves" are/is my favorite poem(s).

At Home: What two poems or stories do you like? Tell a family member and explain your answer using compound subjects in your sentences.

▶ **Critical Thinking**

Name________________ Date__________ **Extend 11**

Combining Sentences: Compound Predicates

First, read all of the sentences. Then choose words from the word box to complete each one. Combine each pair of sentences and then underline the compound predicate. **Answers may vary.**

ate	biked	climb	hiked	fly
photograph	sail	slept	tour	visit

1. Do you want to **visit** France?
   Do you want to **tour** France?
   Do you want to visit and tour France?

2. Will you **fly** there?
   Will you **sail** there?
   Will you fly or sail there?

3. In Paris you can **photograph** the Eiffel Tower.
   In Paris you can **climb** the Eiffel Tower.
   In Paris you can photograph and climb the Eiffel Tower.

4. Mona and her parents **biked** in the countryside.
   Mona and her parents **hiked** in the countryside.
   Mona and her parents biked and hiked in the countryside.

5. They **ate** in an old castle.
   They **slept** in an old castle.
   They ate and slept in an old castle.

At Home: Draw a picture of a place you would like to visit and write a caption for your picture using a compound predicate.

▶ **Critical Thinking**

Name________________ Date__________ **Extend 12**

Mechanics and Usage: Correcting Run-on Sentences

Boris was writing a report on his computer. Then something went wrong. All of his sentences became run-ons. Correct the run-on sentences and rewrite Boris's report. Use separate sentences, compound sentences, or combine subjects or predicates. See how smooth you can make the writing!

> Benjamin Franklin was born in 1706 in Boston, Massachusetts he had many brothers he had many sisters Ben's father taught him how to make candles he taught him how to make soap the job was not fun for Ben Ben went to work for his brother James in his print shop he learned all about type he learned how to run a printing press after Ben was grown, he opened his own printing shop he married he had two sons William was one son. Francis was one son Francis died of smallpox when he was four Ben published *Poor Richard's Almanack* He invented the Franklin Stove He invented the lightning rod. He . . .

Answers will vary. Possible responses are given.

Benjamin Franklin was born in 1706 in Boston, Massachusetts. He had many brothers and sisters. Ben's father taught him how to make candles and soap. The job was not fun for Ben. Ben went to work for his brother James in his print shop. He learned all about type, and he learned how to run a printing press. After Ben was grown, he opened his own printing shop. He married and had two sons, William and Francis. Francis died of smallpox when he was four. Ben published *Poor Richard's Almanack*. He invented the Franklin Stove and the lightning rod. He . . .

At Home: Underline the complete predicate(s) in the sentences you wrote.

▶ **Critical Thinking**

Name________________________ Date____________ **Extend** 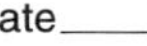 13

Mixed Review

Rewrite the following paragraphs with corrections on the lines below. Join some sentences, and separate others. Make sure each sentence has a complete subject and a complete predicate.

Glenna Goodacre is a sculptor she is also a mother and a grandmother. She designed the first coin to honor a Native American woman.

The woman is Sacajawea. A Shoshone guide who went with Lewis and Clark on part of their journey to the Pacific. The coin. Shows Sacajawea carrying her young son he went on the voyage, too.

Can you tell why the coin is very different from others. Sacajawea's face looks out directly at us other coins show people's profiles.

Glenna Goodacre is the first woman ever to design a U.S. coin now isn't that amazing.

Glenna Goodacre is a sculptor. She is also a mother and a grandmother. She designed the first coin to honor a Native American woman.

The woman is Sacajawea, a Shoshone guide who went with Lewis and Clark on part of their journey to the Pacific. The coin shows Sacajawea carrying her young son. He went on the voyage, too.

Can you tell why the coin is very different from others? Sacajawea's face looks out directly at us. Other coins show people's profiles.

Glenna Goodacre is the first woman ever to design a U.S. coin. Now, isn't that amazing?

At Home: Look closely at any coin, both the head and tail sides. Write a description of the coin. Use complete sentences and correct punctuation. Show your work to a family member.

▶ Critical Thinking

Name________________________ Date____________ **Extend** 14

Common Errors: Sentence Fragments and Run-On Sentences

Correct sentence fragments and run-on sentences by rewriting the directions below.

For the Birds

To make a bird feeder. You will need an empty half-gallon milk carton, tape. Scissors, string, and birdseed. Use dish soap and warm water to wash out the carton then dry it with a towel tape the top closed. Cut out. The two sides of the carton, leaving about an inch around the sides. And about two inches along the bottom. Carefully punch two holes in the top of the carton run the string through the holes so that the feeder can hang from a tree branch. Fill the bottom. Of the carton with birdseed. Hang the feeder in a tree be sure to keep it filled up.

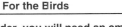

For the Birds

To make a bird feeder, you will need an empty half-gallon milk carton, tape, scissors, string, and birdseed. Use dish soap and warm water to wash out the carton. Then dry it with a towel. Tape the top closed. Cut out two sides of the carton, leaving about an inch around the sides and about two inches along the bottom. Carefully punch two holes in the top of the carton. Run the string through the holes so that the feeder can hang from a tree branch. Fill the bottom of the carton with birdseed. Hang the feeder in a tree. Be sure to keep it filled up.

At Home: Do some after-school bird watching. Keep notes about the birds that you observe and see if you can identify them. Be sure to use complete sentences in your notes.

▶ Critical Thinking

Name______________________ Date__________ **Extend 15**

Study Skills: Note-Taking and Summarizing

Leandra and Dale are working on a science report on wind. They go to the library and read an article entitled "Blowing over the Earth," which presents important information on their report topic.

Read the article. Then help Leandra and Dale by taking notes about the main idea and supporting details on the note card shown below.

It cools you on a hot day and brings on a chill in winter. It is the earth's breath, which is known as wind. Wind is no more than air in motion. The motion is caused by differences in air temperature and air pressure. The warmth of the sun reflecting off the earth heats the air.

Air is made up of molecules. Heat causes air molecules to rise. As the warmed molecules of air rise, cooler molecules of air rush in to take their place.

The direction of the wind and the speed at which it moves affect our weather. You can tell from which direction the wind is moving by observing a flag or a wind vane.

When weather forecasters tell us "there are west winds," this means that the wind is traveling from west to east.

How do scientists measure the wind's strength and speed? They use the Beaufort Wind Scale, invented by a British admiral over a century ago. This scale helps to demonstrate the strength of the wind. Number 1 indicates a calm wind moving less than 1 mile per hour, like the movement of smoke rising into the sky. Number 12 indicates a destructive wind greater than 73 miles per hour, like the winds in a hurricane.

Main Idea: wind is air in motion

Supporting details: (1) temperature and air pressure cause air to move; hot air rises, cool air takes its place (2) a blowing flag or wind vane tells us from where a wind is coming (3) Beaufort Scale of Wind measures wind strength and speed from 1 (1 mile per hour) to 12 (over 73 miles per hour, as in a hurricane).

At Home: Use the notes you took on the article about wind and write a summary.

▶ **Critical Thinking**

Name______________________ Date__________ **Extend 16**

Vocabulary: Time-Order Words

Rearrange the following sentences in good time order.

1. Then, she thinks about where the story takes place.
2. When an artist designs a picture book, she does things step by step.
3. Finally, she decides which picture should go with each
4. Maybe the very last decision is choosing paint or crayon or ink to draw the pictures.
5. As soon as she begins laying out the book, she decides if the picture should show a character close up or far away.
6. Next, she thinks about the characters.
7. First, she reads the story that the author wrote.
8. Perhaps she will choose to show a bird's-eye view, looking down from someplace high.

1. When an artist designs a picture book, she does things step by step.
2. First, she reads the story that the author wrote.
3. Next, she thinks about the characters.
4. Then, she thinks about where the story takes place.
5. Finally, she decides which picture should go with each page of text.
6. As soon as she begins laying out the book, she decides if the picture should show a character close up or far away.
7. Perhaps she will choose to show a bird's-eye view, looking down from someplace high.
8. Maybe the very last decision is that of choosing paint, crayon, or ink to draw the pictures.

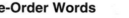

At Home: Tell a family member how time-order words can help you in speaking and writing.

▶ **Critical Thinking**

McGraw-Hill School Division

Name ____________ Date ________ **Extend 17**

Composition: Main Idea

A. Choose a topic sentence for the supporting details listed below. Write the letter of the sentence on the line.

1. __b__ You can visit volcanoes. You can go snorkeling. You can go beach-combing on miles of sandy shore.

a. Outdoor sports are fun.
b. Hawaii is a great vacation spot.
c. Everyone likes going to the beach.

2. __a__ It is interesting. It is challenging. It comes in handy for three meals a day!

a. Cooking is a delicious hobby.
b. Learning a foreign language is something everyone should do.
c. There is nothing dull about learning to play an instrument.

3. __b__ It is exciting to get a closer look at faraway places, and knowing more about the planets can tell us more about how the universe began.

a. Photographs of Jupiter show its moons.
b. Space exploration can help us understand our past.
c. Mercury is the closest planet to the sun.

4. __c__ It includes Lake Tahoe, a year-round vacation spot, and Mt. Whitney, the tallest peak in the continental U.S.

a. The Sierra Nevada is a good place for mountain climbing.
b. The Sierra Nevada is a paradise for skiers.
c. The Sierra Nevada extends down the eastern side of California.

5. __a__ It is famous for its hills, its cable cars, Fisherman's Wharf, sourdough bread, the Golden Gate Bridge, and the Forty-Niners.

a. San Francisco is a distinctive city.
b. San Francisco has a beautiful skyline.
c. The Bay Bridge connects San Francisco to Oakland.

B. Look at the picture of the Statue of Liberty.
Write a topic sentence and two supporting details about it.

At Home: Choose a topic from this page, and add three more detail sentences.

▶ **Critical Thinking**

Name ____________ Date ________ **Extend 18**

Nouns

Write each word from the box under the correct heading in the chart.

actor	Asia	bamboo	wrestler	chopsticks
emperor	fan	kite	island	Japan
Kyoto	lantern	puppeteer	rice	sandals
samurai	lord	tea	Tokyo	kimono
	yen		cherry-blossoms	

Nouns		
PERSON	**PLACE**	**THING**
actor	Asia	bamboo
wrestler	Japan	cherry-blossoms
emperor	Kyoto	chopsticks
lord	Tokyo	fan
puppeteer	island	kite
samurai		kimono
		lantern
		rice
		sandals
		tea
		yen

At Home: Think of other words that you could add to the chart. Explain why they belong where they do.

▶ **Critical Thinking**

Name________________ Date__________ **Extend 19**

Singular and Plural Nouns

Each answer to the puzzle is a plural noun. To complete the puzzle, add *s* or *es* to the nouns in the word box.

acorn	branch	bush	finch	flower
pea	radish	reed	syrup	weed

Across

1. Seeds are formed here.
2. These are the woody parts of a tree that grow from the trunk.
5. These are made from sap.
8. These are unwanted plants.

Down

1. These are birds.
2. These are shrubs.
3. Squirrels store them.
4. These are grasses that grow in wet places.
6. These are vegetables with a sharp taste.
7. These come from pods.

1 flowers
2 branches
5 syrups
8 weeds

1 finches
2 bushes
3 acorns
4 reeds
6 radishes
7 peas

At Home: Make up your own crossword puzzle or word search using the words in the word box.

▶ **Critical Thinking**

McGraw-Hill Language Arts Grade 4, Unit 2, Nouns, pages 90–91

Name________________ Date__________ **Extend 20**

Nouns ending with *y*

Write the plural noun that describes each picture.

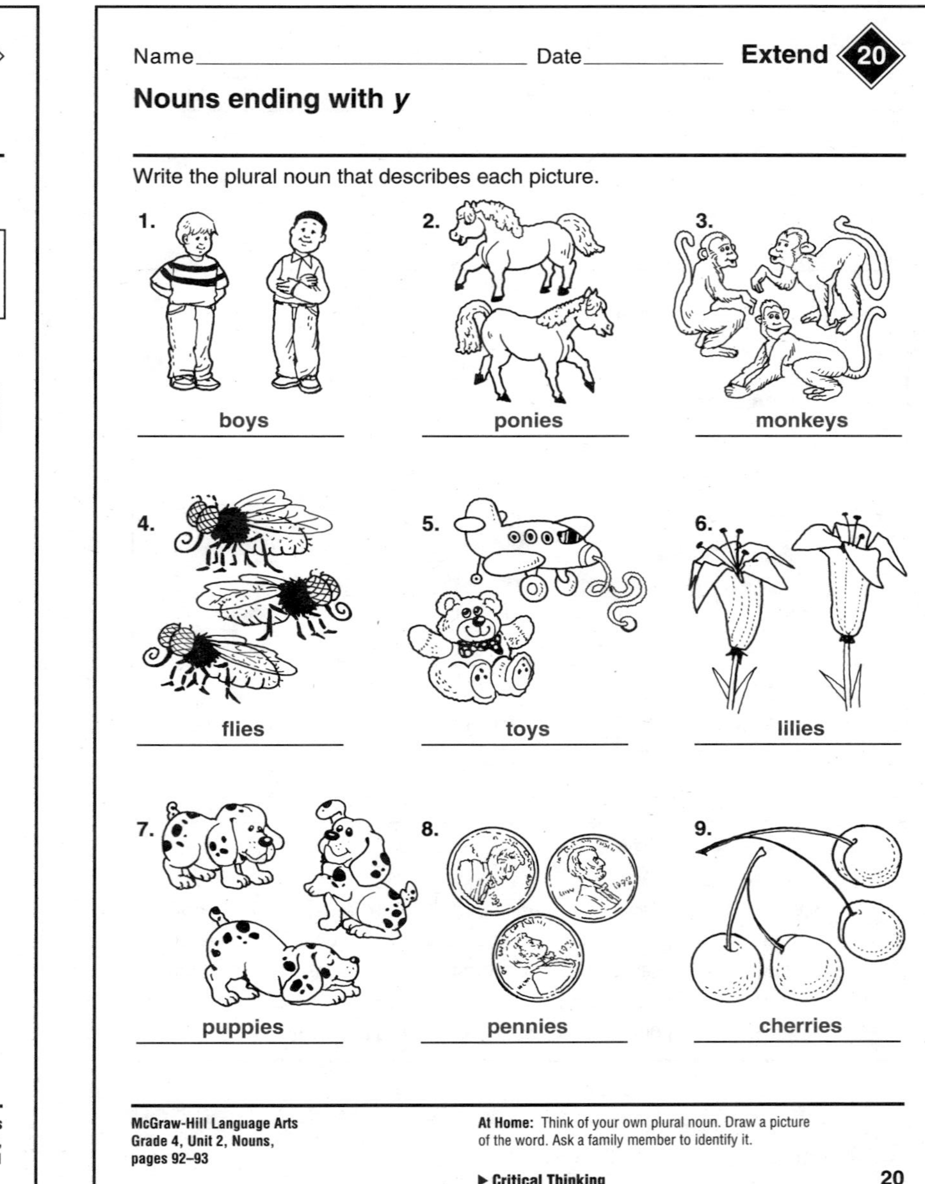

McGraw-Hill Language Arts Grade 4, Unit 2, Nouns, pages 92–93

At Home: Think of your own plural noun. Draw a picture of the word. Ask a family member to identify it.

▶ **Critical Thinking**

McGraw-Hill School Division

Name________________________ Date____________ **Extend 21**

More Plural Nouns

To complete the puzzle, write the plural noun of the following words.

Across	Down
3. scissors	**1.** deer
6. mouse	**2.** moose
8. woman	**4.** child
9. ox	**5.** sheep
10. tooth	**7.** man

						1 d				
						e				
					2 m	e				
3 s	4 c	i	5 s	s	o	r	s			
	h		h		o					
6 m	i	c	e		s					7 m
	l		e		e					e
	d		p			8 w	o	m	e	n
	r			9 o	x	e	n			
10 t	e	e	t	h						
	n									

At Home: How many of the plural nouns in this puzzle keep the same spelling as the singular form of the noun?

▶ **Critical Thinking**

Name________________________ Date____________ **Extend 22**

Common and Proper Nouns

Correct the following invitation, memo, poster, and schedule. Underline letters that should be capitalized with three lines. (b)

Come to a party
for
brenda milkens
friday, july 7, 2000
8:00 P. M.

MEMO

From: jim bennett
Re: Meeting next thurs.

I got your note last week. Sorry I can't come to the meeting next thursday. I'll be in chicago at a sales meeting.

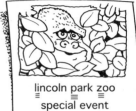

lincoln park zoo
special event

gorilla house opening

entertainment
food games
memorial day
may 29
Rain date: june 3

Leave		Arrive	
detroit	9:00 P.M.	kansas city	11:00 P.M.
grand rapids	7:00 A.M.	milwaukee	8:00 A.M.
st. clare shores	6:00 P.M.	new york	11:30 P.M.

At Home: Design a poster to advertise an upcoming school event.

▶ **Critical Thinking**

Name ________________ Date __________ **Extend** 

Mechanics and Usage: Capitalization

Pretend you are Doreen and you wrote this letter to your grandmother. Add capital letters where they belong.

> Dear Granny,
>
> I can't wait till we come see you on Thanksgiving. My teacher, Miss Robinson, showed us how to make turkeys with apples and toothpicks. I made one for you.
>
> Mister Phillips asked me to walk his dog Sparkles next Saturday and Sunday. He is taking a trip to California. He wants to visit Yosemite National Park and Knott's Berry Farm.
>
> Dad took me to Doctor Driller last Monday after school. I didn't have any cavities. Hooray! Then Dad drove me down Mulberry Street. The Cattail Nature Center was open. We saw bees in a hive. Miss Fremont gave a talk about how honey is made.
>
> I must study for my English test tomorrow. I just finished reading *Little House in the Big Woods*, by Laura Ingalls Wilder.
>
> Love,
> Doreen

At Home: Substitute new proper nouns for those used in the letter above.

▶ Critical Thinking

McGraw-Hill Language Arts
Grade 4, Unit 2, Nouns,
pages 98–99

Name ________________ Date __________ **Extend** 24

Mixed Review

A. Name each picture in each pair. Write both singular and plural nouns.

1. cherry — cherries
2. child — children
3. monkey — monkeys

B. Underline the proper nouns on the following calendar book and address book.

Calendar Book

February holidays:
Groundhog Day
My Birthday
Valentine's Day
Presidents' Day

Address Book

My dentist
Dr. D. Beadley
1765 East Milford Ave.
Sharon, CT 06069
860-555-5555
My lawyer
Sara Brentwell
345 College Ave.
Essex, VT 05452
878-555-5555

McGraw-Hill Language Arts
Grade 4, Unit 2, Mixed Review,
pages 100–101

At Home: List all the names and addresses of five different friends or relatives. Use correct punctuation. These listings can be part of your personal address book, if you wish.

▶ Critical Thinking

Name____________ Date________ **Extend 25**

Singular Possessive Nouns

Rewrite the paragraph. Use singular possessive nouns to replace the underlined fragments. Remember to include an apostrophe.

The Tale of Michael

I found the joke book that belongs to Jake at the house of my grandfather. The cane that belongs to my grandfather was left at the country store that belongs to Clem. Clem came to our house in the car that belongs to his mother and left the cane and a frozen pizza from the deli that is owned by Pino. I returned the joke book to Jake and borrowed a CD that belongs to his sister. Jake asked to borrow the radio that belongs to my older brother. My brother said he needed the radio to take to his job on the farm belonging to Dutton. Mom said that the corn from last week was sweet and delicious.

Michael's Tale

I found Jake's joke book at my grandfather's house. My grandfather's cane was left at Clem's country store. Clem came to our house in his mother's car and left the cane and a frozen pizza from Pino's deli. I returned the joke book to Jake and borrowed his sister's CD. Jake asked to borrow my older brother's radio. My brother said he needed the radio to take to his job on Dutton's farm. Mom said that last week's corn was sweet and delicious.

At Home: Describe a country scene. Use singular and possessive nouns.

Name____________ Date________ **Extend 26**

Plural Possessive Nouns

Mark an X on each plural possessive noun that is not written correctly. Then write each word correctly on the lines at the bottom of the page.

Dear Diary:

Yesterday, Amy and I took five three-year-olds to the playground. Two boys pretended to be super-heroes. The boys yelling made me hold my ears. Three girls had a fight over some cement trucks. I dried two of the girls tears and suggested how the three of them could play together. Finally, they were happy.

Then two small dogs came running and barking around the kids kickball game. The dogs barking stopped the game. The dogs owners came running onto the field. "We are sorry," they said. "Our four-year-old removed the pooches leashes from their collars."

At snack time, three older kids spilled their juice right onto two boys sweaters. The boys tears flowed this time. We wiped off the juice, and all was A-OK once again. What a tiring day!

1. **boys' yelling**
2. **girls' tears**
3. **kids' kickball game**
4. **dogs' barking**
5. **dogs' owners**
6. **pooches' leashes**
7. **boys' sweaters**
8. **boys' tears**

At Home: Do you think the writer of this diary entry enjoys volunteering? Tell why or why not.

Name______________ Date________ **Extend 27**

Combining Sentences: Nouns

Complete the following old tale. Use compound subjects and compound objects. Remember to use *and* or *or*. **Answers will vary. Possible answers are given.**

One day John **and/or Drew** stole a pig from their neighbors Bess **and Kyle**. They took the pig home. **John and Drew** looked out the window and saw **Bess and Kyle** coming. Quickly John put the pig in a crib. John got out a blanket **or a hat**. He put it on the pig. He waited for **Bess and/or Kyle**.

"What is the matter with the baby, John?" Bess asked.

"The baby has measles **and fever**," said John. You cannot see him. The doctor said the measles will go inside the baby. The doctor said this would make the baby turn pink."

Bess **and Kyle** stared at the crib.

Then **Kyle or Bess** reached down and uncovered the baby.

"Don't blame me if the baby turned into a pig," said John.

"I will take the pig home," said Bess. "I will take good care of the pig."

"Oink!" said the pig.

At Home: Write a title for this folk tale.

Name______________ Date________ **Extend 28**

Mechanics and Usage: Abbreviations

Use abbreviations to complete a February school calendar. Write the name of the month and abbreviate the days of the week. Add entries with abbreviations for each day shown below. **Answers will vary. Possible answers are given.**

Feb. 4: Meet with Mister Collins 3:30
9: Governor McDonald visits Grades 5–6
11: Doctor Hernandez visits Grade 3
14: School closed for Presidents' Day
23: Grade 3 visits Senator Smith
24: River Street Conservation Society meeting 5:30
29: Chess Club plans April contest

February

Sun.	Mon.	Tues.	Wed.	Thurs.	Fri.	Sat.
		1	2	3	4 Meet with Mr. Collins 3:30	5
6	7	8	9 Gov. McDonald visits Grades 5–6	10	11 Dr. Hernandez visits Grade 3	12
13	14 School closed for Pres. Day	15	16	17	18	19
20	21	22	23 Grade 3 visits Sen. Smith	24 River St. Conservation Society meeting 5:30	25	26
27	28	29 Chess Club plans Apr. contest				

At Home: Why are calendars important to us? Write a few sentences to explain your answer.

Name__________ Date______ **Extend 29**

Mixed Review

A. Combine the following sentences. Underline the nouns in each new sentence.

1. I will send a letter to my teacher. I will send a letter to the insect expert.

I will send a letter to my teacher and the insect expert.

2. We will find out about ticks. We will find out about insects.

We will find out about ticks and insects.

B. There was a computer glitch, and this insect expert's letter needs some fixing. Commas and capitals and other punctuation need to be added. Correct the grammar mistakes. Watch out for possessive nouns!

natural history museum
New York, Ny 10023
Jan 5, 2004

Ms liz Randolph
467 Clinton ave.
Carrboro, NC 17510

Dear Liz,

Your brothers argument is the correct one. A tick is not an insect. A ticks eight legs is a big clue. This makes it an arthropod, just like a spider. A tick has no wings, but an insect does. Ticks bodies are short and round without any segments. An insects body has three distinct parts. A wood tick is very tiny. It lives in the woods. It sucks the blood of deer and other animals. When the tick has not eaten, its body is flat, soft, and elastic. After it has eaten, its body swells.

Some ticks carry disease so don't handle them. If you have a pet that gets ticks, take it to a veterinarian. He or she will know what to do.

sincerely,
Jeremy douglas

At Home: Write sentences about insects. Use compound subjects such as *ticks and mites*. Share your work with a family member.

▶ **Critical Thinking**

Name__________ Date______ **Extend 30**

Common Errors: Plurals and Possessives

Read the letter below. Rewrite the letter, correcting the mistakes made with plural nouns and possessive nouns.

Dear Aunt Bess,

Thank you for sending me the easel and paint's. I have already painted three watercolor's, and I am working on another. One is of a birds nest in the tree outside my moms' office window. I also have signed up for some arts' and craft's classes' at the Childrens' Museum. My teachers husband is going to set up weekend art workshop's, and my friends' and I might be able to take them. Plus, our next door neighbors studio is mine to use while she is out of town. Your gift's will help me find success with all of these activitie's!

Your's truly,
Terry

Dear Aunt Bess,

Thank you for sending me the easel and paints. I have already painted three watercolors, and I am working on another. One is of a bird's nest in the tree outside my mom's office window. I also have signed up for some arts and crafts classes at the Children's Museum. My teacher's husband is going to set up weekend art workshops, and my friends and I might be able to take them. Plus, our next door neighbor's studio is mine to use while she is out of town. Your gifts will help me find success with all of these activities!

Yours truly,
Terry

At Home: When have you received a special gift? Write a thank-you note to a relative. Be sure to punctuate plural nouns and plural possessives correctly.

▶ **Critical Thinking**

Name________________ Date________ **Extend 31**

Study Skills: Parts of a Book

Althea loved information and often researched topics that interested her. Her last research topic was sound and light energy. She kept note cards and organized them by the pages of books on which she found the information. Unfortunately, Althea's new puppy knocked the piles of cards off of her bed. Now they are all mixed up on the floor of her room.

Help Althea organize her cards into these five categories: **title page, copyright page, table of contents, index,** and **glossary.** Write where they belong on the lines.

1. copyright © 1999 — copyright page
2. by Anita Pohwerz, Ph.D. — title page
3. Sound Waves 4–7, 18 — index
4. Chapter 3 What Makes a Rainbow? .... 19 — table of contents
5. reflection [ri-flek-shən] the return of light or sound waves from a surface — glossary
6. Chapter 1 Waves of Energy............... 3 — table of contents
7. lux [ləks] a unit of measure for the brightness of light — glossary
8. The Book of Energy — title page
9. wave [wāv] a disturbance that travels through matter or space — glossary
10. Science Publishing Company, Inc. San Francisco • Chicago • Boston — title page
11. Rainbows 19–25, 27, 42 — index
12. Index.............116 — table of contents
13. Neon 67–72 with laser production 70 — index
14. Chapter 12 Problems of Noise Pollution.......88 — table of contents
15. pitch [pich] the highness or lowness of a sound — glossary

At Home: Make up another card for each pile of Althea's cards.

McGraw-Hill Language Arts Grade 4, Unit 2, Study Skills, pages 120–121

▶ **Critical Thinking**

Name________________ Date________ **Extend 32**

Vocabulary: Compound Words

Each answer to the crossword puzzle is a compound word. Can you figure out its theme? **weather**

Across

1. The shining light of the sun
3. He predicts the weather.
4. They fall from the sky.
6. You can get this when you're at the beach.
7. Every one has six points but no two are exactly alike.
8. You wear it to keep from getting wet.
9. This warns ships of fog.

Down

1. A fall of snow
2. He usually has a carrot nose.
5. A sudden, heavy rain
7. The light of the sun

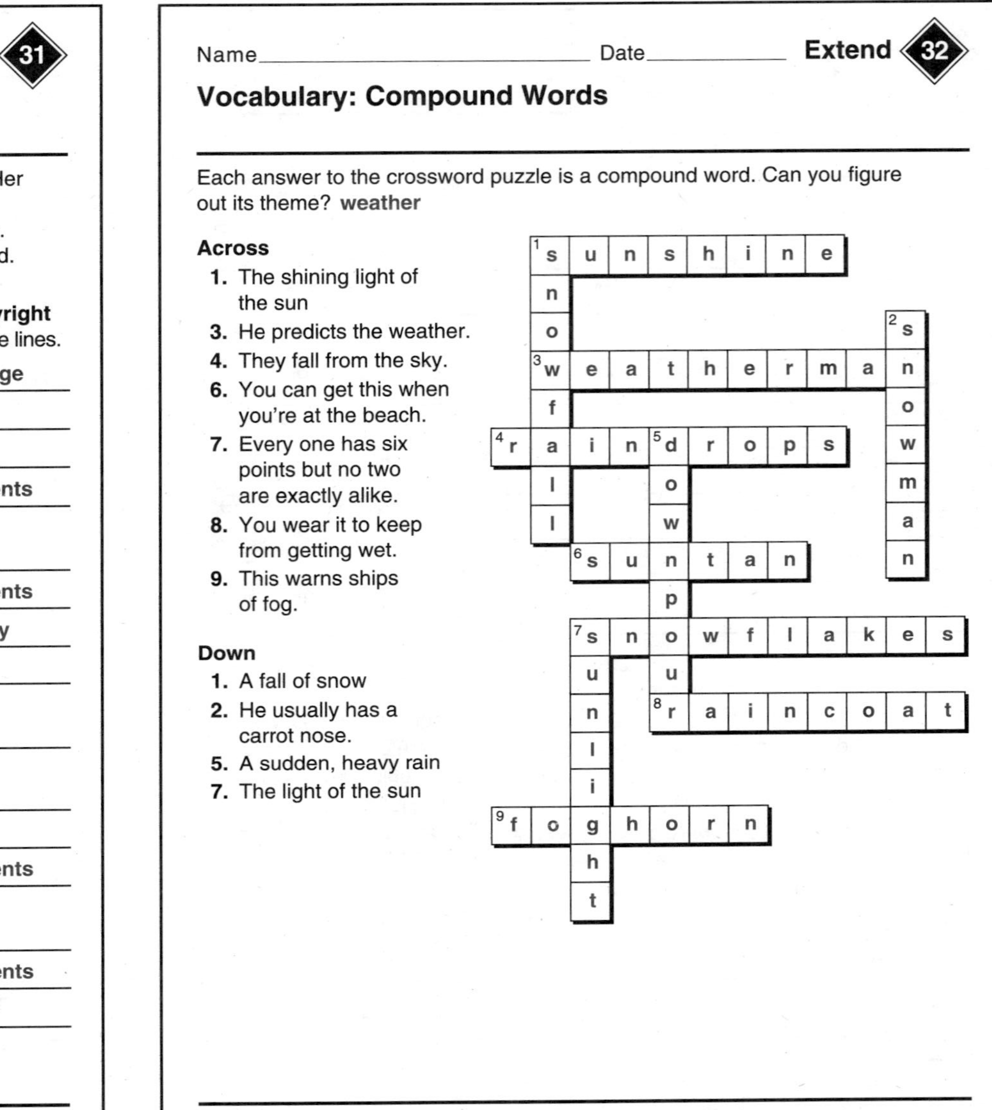

McGraw-Hill Language Arts Grade 4, Unit 2, Vocabulary, pages 122–123

At Home: List other compound words relating to the theme above and create your own crossword puzzle with them.

▶ **Critical Thinking**

Name______________ Date________ **Extend 33**

Composition Skills: Writing Descriptions

Use vivid details and words that appeal to the five senses to write a sentence that describes each thing below. Be sure your sentence creates a clear mental picture. **Answers will vary. Possible answers are given.**

1. a cold day
   My teeth chattered as I stood in the snow.
2. a strong wind
   Blasts of wind battered the tops of the trees.
3. a new bicycle
   The chrome glittered like a silver star.
4. bright moonlight
   The moon cast a bright glow around the yard.
5. a glowing sunset
   The orange sun seemed to melt and ooze across the dark blue sky.
6. a busy airport
   People rushed and bustled through the crowded terminal.
7. a traffic jam
   The row of cars inched along like a line of marching turtles.
8. a jolly baby
   The rosy baby giggled, holding her toes in her chubby little hands.
9. a friendly dog
   The dog ran up, his tongue lolling out in a loopy, goopy grin.
10. students in a quiet classroom
    The scratch of pencils on paper was the only sound.
11. students in a cafeteria
    The cafeteria buzzed like a hive of bees.
12. a boat on a lake
    The boat bobbed like a cork in a bucket of water.

At Home: How does the weather affect your mood? Write a description of the weather and include details about how it makes you feel.

▶ **Critical Thinking**

Name______________ Date________ **Extend 34**

Action Verbs

What kind of jokes did Albert Einstein, the great scientist, make?

To find the answer, write the action verb in each sentence. Then unscramble the circled letters and write them on the lines below.

1. Bill often works late into the night. (w) o r (k) s
2. He illustrates children's books. (i) l l u s t r a t e s
3. Sometimes he paints with a tiny brush. p a i n t (s)
4. Often he mixes several colors together. m i x (e) s
5. Bill also carves wood. (c) (a) r v e s
6. He designs totem poles and Kachina dolls. d e s i g n s
7. He decorates them with Indian symbols. d e (c) o (r) a t e s
8. Sometimes he sells his artwork. s e l l s
9. He often exhibits his work in a museum. e x h i b i t s
10. Sometimes he visits children in schools. v i s i t (s)

w i s e c r a c k s

At Home: Work with a family member. Form at least two more action verbs with the circled letters. *Ski* is one possibility.

▶ **Critical Thinking**

Name ______________ Date ________ **Extend 35**

Verb Tenses

Rewrite the sentences from the following paragraph in the correct time order—past, present, and future. **Order may vary for present and future tense sentences.**

My album is almost full. That will be great! Maybe someday I will take a photography class. When I was younger, I loved to look at photos of me as a baby. I enjoy taking pictures of my friends. Snap, snap, my camera goes. Everyone says I was a cutie pie! When I am older, I will take pictures of places I visit. I will learn how to develop my own film. Now I have my own camera.

1. **When I was younger, I loved to look at photos of me as a baby.**
2. **Everyone says I was a cutie pie!**
3. **Now I have my own camera.**
4. **I enjoy taking pictures of my friends.**
5. **Snap, snap, my camera goes.**
6. **My album is almost full.**
7. **When I am older, I will take pictures of places I visit.**
8. **Maybe someday I will take a photography class.**
9. **I will learn how to develop my own film.**
10. **That will be great!**

At Home: Do you have a favorite photograph in your family album? Write a story about it.

▶ **Critical Thinking**

Name ______________ Date ________ **Extend 36**

Subject-Verb Agreement

Olga recently arrived from Europe. She is learning English fast, but has some difficulty with verb tenses. She wrote the following in her diary after a tough day. Help Olga. Cross out the incorrect verb and write the correct verb form above it.

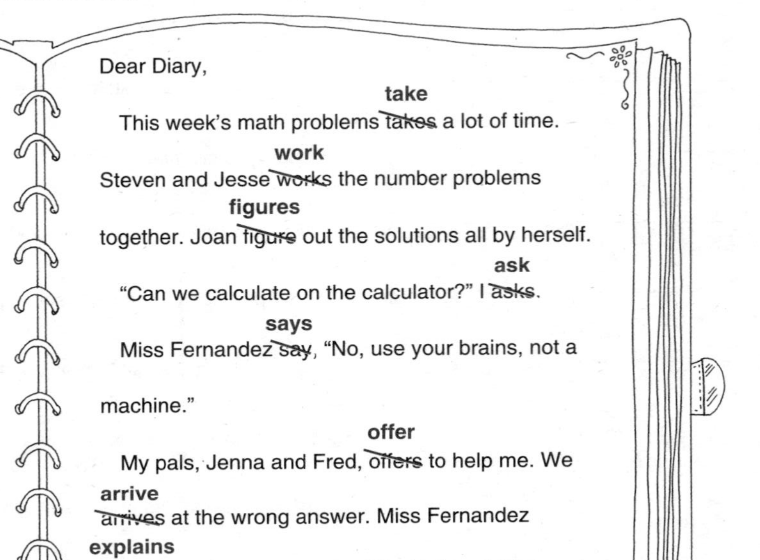

Dear Diary,

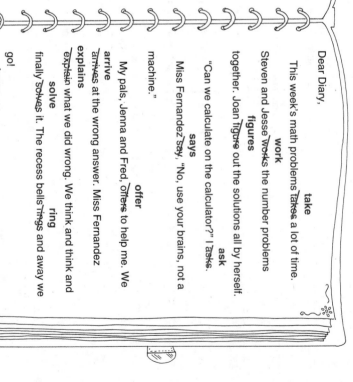

This week's math problems ~~takes~~ **take** a lot of time. Steven and Jesse ~~works~~ **work** the number problems together. Joan ~~figure~~ **figures** out the solutions all by herself.

"Can we calculate on the calculator?" I ~~asks~~ **ask**.

Miss Fernandez ~~say~~ **says**, "No, use your brains, not a machine."

My pals, Jenna and Fred, ~~offers~~ **offer** to help me. We ~~arrives~~ **arrive** at the wrong answer. Miss Fernandez ~~explain~~ **explains** what we did wrong. We think and think and finally ~~solves~~ **solve** it. The recess bells ~~rings~~ **ring** and away we go!

I ~~hopes~~ **hope** tomorrow is a better day.

At Home: Locate a country in Europe on a map and list three of its cities and two of its rivers.

▶ **Critical Thinking**

Name________________ Date__________ Extend 37

Spelling Present-Tense and Past-Tense Verbs

Complete the puzzle by writing the verb tense shown in parentheses in the puzzle. Use the puzzle clue.

I (hurry)	(past)	**4 across**	I (whisper)	(present)	**3 down**
You (scurry)	(past)	**2 down**	You (shop)	(past)	**5 down**
We (try)	(past)	**9 across**	They (ship)	(past)	**5 across**
She (wonder)	(present)	**6 across**	We (plop)	(past)	**7 down**
He (yell)	(present)	**1 across**	You (drop)	(past)	**8 across**

1 across: yells
2 down: scurried
3 down: whispers
4 across: hurried
5 across: shipped
5 down: shopped
6 across: wonders
7 down: plopped
8 across: dropped
9 across: tried

At Home: Make up a poem using words in the puzzle. Recite your poem to a family member.

▶ **Critical Thinking**

Name________________ Date__________ Extend 38

Mechanics and Usage: Commas in a Series

Pretend your younger brother or sister wrote the following report for class. He or she asked you to proofread it. Read the paragraphs and add commas where needed.

Do you know what the closest star to Earth is? Yes it is the sun. All the other stars are very far away. Some of the brightest "stars" are actually planets. Venus Mars Jupiter and Saturn can be seen without a telescope. There are red stars yellow stars white stars and blue-white stars. Blue-white stars are the hottest the red stars are the coolest and the others are in between.

Most constellations are named after animals ancient gods or heroes. See if you can find Orion Taurus the Bull and the Big Dipper in a book. Then share your information with your parents a brother a sister or a friend.

Do you know what the closest star to Earth is? Yes, it is the sun. All the other stars are very far away. Some of the brightest "stars" are actually planets. Venus, Mars, Jupiter, and Saturn can be seen without a telescope. There are red stars, yellow stars, white stars, and blue-white stars. Blue-white stars are the hottest, the red stars are the coolest, and the others are in between.

Most constellations are named after animals, ancient gods, or heroes. See if you can find Orion, Taurus the Bull, and the Big Dipper in the sky. Then share your information with your parents, a brother, a sister, or a friend.

At Home: Draw a picture of one of the constellations named above. Then tell a family member about it.

▶ **Critical Thinking**

Name __________ Date __________ **Extend 39**

Mixed Review

A. Write the correct verb tenses as indicated in the parentheses. Then write a sentence with the verb. **Challenge:** Try to keep your sentences on one topic, such as art or sports. **Sentences will vary.**

1. jump (past) **jumped**
2. practice (future) **will practice**
3. pasted (present) **paste, pastes**
4. create (past) **created**
5. hurry (past) **hurried**
6. watch (past) **watched**
7. stop (past) **stopped**
8. carried (future) **will carry**
9. will try (past) **tried**
10. grin (past) **grinned**

B. Rewrite each sentence. Add a verb and commas where they belong. **Answers may vary.**

11. I ______ to the sixth-grade class the kids in the library and our principal.
I spoke to the sixth grade class, the kids in the library, and our principal.

12. Everyone said we ______ soap towels wax and a hose for the car wash.
Everyone said we will need/need soap, towels, wax, and a hose for the car wash.

13. Let's ______ if we can hold it on one of the following dates: Saturday the seventh, the fourteenth, or the twenty-first.
Let's ask if we can hold it on one of the following dates: Saturday the seventh, the fourteenth, or the twenty-first.

At Home: Observe a family member in the kitchen preparing food. List as many verbs as you can that describe the action being done. For example: *cook, mixing, marinated.*

▶ **Critical Thinking**

McGraw-Hill Language Arts Grade 4, Unit 3, Mixed Review, pages 180–181

Name __________ Date __________ **Extend 40**

Main Verbs and Helping Verbs

Pretend you are a reporter for your school newspaper. You are covering the orchestra rehearsal and taking notes. Locate and write each helping verb and main verb below. Then draw one line under the helping verb and draw two lines under each main verb.

The school orchestra is rehearsing in the auditorium. Mr. Ames will conduct the concert tonight. I can hear the strings. The violinist is making a squeaky sound. The boy playing cello is humming with the music. A girl with her flute is running toward her seat. The trumpet and trombone players were talking a second ago. Mr. Ames is tapping his baton. I bet he will scold them.

"You should arrive on time," he said to the girl.

"Boys, I will need quiet," he said.

I shall attend the concert with my parents. My cousin Ted would enjoy the music, I think. I could ask him to join us. I will write my review for the school newspaper tomorrow morning.

1.	**is rehearsing**	6.	**is running**	11.	**will need**
2.	**will conduct**	7.	**were talking**	12.	**shall attend**
3.	**can hear**	8.	**is tapping**	13.	**would enjoy**
4.	**is making**	9.	**will scold**	14.	**could ask**
5.	**is humming**	10.	**should arrive**	15.	**will write**

McGraw-Hill Language Arts Grade 4, Unit 3, Verbs, pages 182–183

At Home: What musical instrument do you play or would like to play? Write about it using main and helping verbs.

▶ **Critical Thinking**

Name_______________ Date_______ **Extend 41**

Using Helping Verbs

Here is a riddle: What travels around the world but stays in a corner?

To find the answer, first circle the helping verb and the main verb in each sentence. Then unscramble the underlined letters. Write each letter on a line below.

1. When I was your age, I (had received) my share of bumps and bruises.
2. On the soccer field, my big toe (was stepped) on.
3. The doctor (had looked) at an X-ray; it was only a bruise.
4. One day, I (was running) on the sidewalk.
5. Then oops! I realized I (had tripped) and cut my knee.
6. I (had walked) around with a bandage for a week.
7. For years, Dad and my uncle (were trying) to get me to believe that a gorilla came to visit me when I was two.
8. I (have) never (believed) those jokers!
9. When I was five, I told Mom that an elephant (had smashed) my broken toy.
10. Kids (have swapped) stories like that for generations.

a s t a m p

At Home: Make up a riddle. Tell it to a family member.

McGraw-Hill Language Arts
Grade 4, Unit 3, Verbs,
pages 184–185

▶ Critical Thinking

Name_______________ Date_______ **Extend 42**

Linking Verbs

Read each sentence. Underline the linking verb. Circle the noun or adjective in the predicate. Then replace the noun or adjective with a synonym. **Answers will vary. Possible responses are shown.**

1. Our class is (excited.) **nervous**
2. Our spring play will be (funny.) **amusing, comical**
3. The characters in it are (silly.) **funny, ridiculous**
4. Samantha is the (narrator.) **storyteller, reader**
5. My best pal, Mohammed, is (tall.) **big, lanky**
6. Deciding who plays the giant was (easy.) **simple, uncomplicated, a cinch**
7. The stage in the auditorium is (huge.) **big, enormous, gigantic**
8. Carrie says her stomach is (jumpy.) **sick, nervous, jittery**
9. I am not (nervous.) **scared, tense**
10. I am the (one) who pulls the curtains. **person, child, boy, girl**
11. The curtains are (shiny.) **glossy**
12. Our teacher is (proud) of us. **pleased**
13. Our parents are (happy.) **joyful, glad**

McGraw-Hill Language Arts
Grade 4, Unit 3, Verbs,
pages 186–187

At Home: Write a short description of a scene for a class play. Include linking verbs.

▶ Critical Thinking

McGraw-Hill School Division

Name__________ Date________ **Extend 43**

Using Linking Verbs

Add the correct form of the verb *be* to each sentence. Then find and circle all the forms of the verb *be* in the puzzle below. Look down, across, and diagonally.

Family Fun

Every year during the summer our family members **are** guests at a reunion. Last year there **were** about 75 people. The kids **were/are** different ages, from tiny babies to teens. My cousin Jean **was/is** the oldest. I **was/am** in between her and the babies. I **was** twelve on my last birthday. Everyone **was** always busy doing something. The grown-ups did a lot of talking and cooking. The kids played games. The biggest event **was** the family baseball game. My team won. We **were** all so proud! I wonder where our next reunion **will be**.

w	e	r	e	a	m
a	i	a	m	r	y
m	i	i	i	e	w
a	m	s	i	i	a
s	m	s	a	b	r
a	i	a	a	r	e

At Home: Make up your own word search puzzle with words from the above paragraph. Have a family member solve it.

▶ **Critical Thinking**

Name__________ Date________ **Extend 44**

Irregular Verbs

Use the irregular forms of the verbs in parentheses to complete each sentence.

1. I (eat) **ate** a snack after school.
2. Then I (go) **went** to my art class at the recreation center.
3. I (bring) **brought** along some of my favorite paintings.
4. I (make) **made** one using crayon and watercolors.
5. "Have you (see) **seen** Max's picture?" Mrs. Applebaum asked everyone. "It's wonderful."
6. Maria quietly (run) **ran** into the classroom, trying to be unnoticed.
7. Of course, Ms. Applebaum (see) **saw** her.
8. She (do) **did** not say anything to Maria.
9. She just (give) **gave** her a stern look.
10. "I had (make) **made** some slides to show you last week," said my teacher.
11. "I had (go) **gone** to the library to borrow some books."
12. "I (come) **came** across this book on the Impressionists, and I want to share it with you, too."

At Home: Write a paragraph that continues the story told above. Use irregular verbs in each sentence.

▶ **Critical Thinking**

Name__________ Date________ **Extend 45**

More Irregular Verbs

A. Complete the chart.

Present Tense	Past Tense	With Have/Had
begin	began	begun
bring	brought	brought
draw	drew	drawn
drive	drove	driven
fly	flew	flown
grow	grew	grown
ride	rode	ridden

B. What other irregular verbs might you add to the chart? List them.
Answers will vary. Possible words are shown.

swim	swam	swum
take	took	taken
write	wrote	written

At Home: Play a game with a family member. Start by saying a word from the chart above. Then say, "Name its irregular verb when used with *have* or *had*." The family member answers. Continue by taking turns.

▶ **Critical Thinking**

Name__________ Date________ **Extend 46**

Mechanics and Usage: Contractions with *Not*

Replace two words in each sentence to form a contraction with *not*. Write the new sentence on the lines below.

I do not know what to do for the science fair this year. I have not one clue! If I had not wasted time by talking on the phone to my friend, I may have been further along. I will not do what I did last year. I made an electric circuit that would not work when I set it up. The battery was not working properly.

My parents are not helping me this year. They are not being mean. They just think I need to do it myself. I could not find a book about telescopes. The librarian said she does not know what happened to it. So now I can learn how to make shadow puppets. Do not you think that is a good idea?

I don't know what to do for the science fair this year. I haven't one clue! If I hadn't wasted time by talking on the phone to my friend, I may have been further along. I won't do what I did last year. I made an electric circuit that wouldn't work when I set it up. The battery wasn't working properly.

My parents aren't helping me this year. They aren't being mean. They just think I need to do it myself. I couldn't find a book about telescopes. The librarian said she doesn't know what happened to it. So now I can learn how to make shadow puppets. Don't you think that is a good idea?

At Home: Write a paragraph describing a recent science project. Use contractions.

▶ **Critical Thinking**

Name________________ Date__________ **Extend 47**

Mixed Review

Add the missing verb to each sentence. Then tell what kind of verb you wrote by writing either *action, linking, helping,* or *irregular.*
Some answers may vary.

A. 1. I **am** a good cook. **linking**

2. I went to the store and **bought** some chicken legs. **irregular/action**

3. I **gave** the clerk five dollars. **action/irregular**

4. Then I **bought** some yellow rice. **action/irregular**

5. I **basted** the chicken with barbecue sauce. **action**

6. Mom and Dad **are** on their way home. **linking**

7. My brother Pablo **wants** to make the salad. **action**

8. I **washed** the vegetables for him. **action**

9. Now he **mixes** the oil, vinegar, and garlic for the salad dressing. **action**

10. "You **have** made us very happy," said Mom and Dad. **helping**

B. Underline all the past-tense verbs in the sentences above. **Answers will vary.**

C. On a separate sheet of paper, write a letter to a friend or relative. Explain how to prepare your favorite recipe. Try to include the four kinds of verbs in your writing.

At Home: Find a recipe in a family cookbook. List all the verbs you find in it, and then write what kind of verb each one is. Share your work with a family member.
▶ **Critical Thinking**

Name________________ Date__________ **Extend 48**

Common Errors: Subject-Verb Agreement

A. Pretend you are a newspaper editor. Read the article below. Underline the correct form of the verbs to complete the article.

Bike Expo Next Week

The City and County Safety Committee (is/are) holding a Bicycle Expo. People (bring/brings) their bikes to the mall parking lot on the second Saturday of the month. Volunteers from local agencies (teach/teaches) riders traffic laws. They also (cover/covers) safety rules.

Bike Universe (has/have) donated helmets to the first 15 bicyclists who (come/comes). The bicyclist who (ride/rides) the farthest to get to the expo (receive/receives) a special award. Children under 10 (compete/competes) for t-shirts, streamers, and other prizes. Afternoon activities (include/includes) workshops and races.

Did you know that bike accidents (send/sends) hundreds of children to the hospital every year? However, the Bike Expo (aim/aims) to reduce the number of accidents and serious injuries that (happen/happens) during the summer months by educating people. The scouts from Troop 751 (provide/provides) refreshments. Families (is/are) encouraged to attend.

B. What other events would you plan for a Bike Expo? Write your ideas to add to the article above. Make sure your subjects and verbs agree in each sentence.

____

____

____

____

At Home: What are some bike safety tips that you follow? Write a list of bike safety rules. Be sure that your subjects and verbs agree.
▶ **Critical Thinking**

Name________________ Date__________ **Extend 49**

Study Skills: Card Catalog

Fourth-graders at Whitman Elementary School in New York have created a library with books they have written themselves.

1. Fill in the author and subject cards below for a nonfiction book about bridges by Cynthia Hernandez with the title *How the Brooklyn Bridge Was Built.* This book was illustrated. In 1999 it was published by the Whitman School Press. It has 23 pages, and its call number is 624 H.

author card

624
H
Hernandez, Cynthia.
How the Brooklyn Bridge
Was Built.
New York: Whitman
School Press, © 1999.
23 p.: illus.

subject card

624
H
BRIDGES
Hernandez, Cynthia.
How the Brooklyn Bridge
Was Built.
New York: Whitman
School Press, © 1999.
23 p.: illus.

2. Name other possible subject card headings for this book.
Possible answers: Brooklyn, History, Architecture

3. Make up another book title which might also have a "BRIDGES" subject card.
Answers will vary.

4. Under what letter would you file this book's title card? **H**

At Home: Make up a set of cards (author, subject, and title) for a book you would one day like to write.

▶ **Critical Thinking**

McGraw-Hill Language Arts
Grade 4, Unit 3, Study Skills,
pages 206–207

Name________________ Date__________ **Extend 50**

Vocabulary: Prefixes

Add a prefix from the box to each underlined word to make the sentence make sense.

dis	in	mis	over	pre	re	un

Understanding the Game

Our opponents **mis** understood how tough we could be. We were not as **dis** organized as they thought. We did have **pre** game jitters, but we got over them. We were able to **re** group and get the job done.

Our coach was **over** joyed with our playing. He said that before the game, he was **un** sure we had enough desire to win. But he **re** considered that idea quickly.

I thought I would be **un** lucky and just have to sit on the bench. I was **in** correct. I ended up hitting two runs, which I thought I was **in** capable of doing. You just never know!

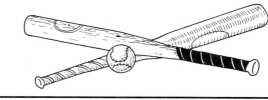

McGraw-Hill Language Arts
Grade 4, Unit 3, Vocabulary,
pages 208–209

At Home: Define *nonfiction* and *nonexistent.* Then find and define two other words that begin with the prefix *non.*

▶ **Critical Thinking**

Name____________________ Date__________ **Extend 51**

Composition: Leads and Endings

Write a strong lead sentence and a strong ending sentence for each topic shown below. **Answers will vary. Possible answers are given.**

1. A Puppy in the House

   Lead **What is brown and cuddly and fits in a basket?**

   Ending **You couldn't ask for a better pal!**

2. Moving to a New Neighborhood

   Lead **It is never easy being the new kid on the block.**

   Ending **It will take some getting used to, but I think I'll like it here.**

3. My Favorite Movie

   Lead **If you like animation, then you will love *Fantasia*.**

   Ending **If you get a chance to see this classic, don't pass it up.**

4. After-School Sports

   Lead **Do you have a lot of free time and extra energy?**

   Ending **You can make the scene when you make the team!**

5. Taking a Trip

   Lead **If you could go anywhere in the world, where would it be?**

   Ending **We were amazed at how much we had packed into seven days.**

6. Doing Volunteer Work

   Lead **There are many worthy charities.**

   Ending **The feeling of satisfaction is very gratifying.**

At Home: Can you think of an after-school job? Make up a flyer that describes your services. Be sure you have a strong lead to grab your readers' attention and strong ending to leave them with a good impression!

▶ **Critical Thinking**

McGraw-Hill Language Arts
Grade 4, Unit 3, Composition Skills, pages 210–211

Name____________________ Date__________ **Extend 52**

Adjectives

Use adjectives from the word box to complete the sentences and the puzzle.

easy	equal	huge	neat
old	stormy	strange	young

Across

1. It was a **stormy** night with heavy rains.
4. Don't you agree that elephants are not small but **huge**?
6. Stewart just cleaned his room, so it is **neat** and orderly.
7. 6 + 10 and 9 + 7 are **equal**.

Down

1. I just learned about the **strange** behavior of puffer fish.
2. The **old** man had lived on his farm for ninety years.
3. Did you know that a kid is a **young** goat?
5. It is **easy** to learn how to use a computer.

1 s	t	2 o	r	m	3 y		
t		l			o		
r		d		4 h	u	g	5 e
a					n		a
6 n	e	a	t		g		s
g							y
7 e	q	u	a	l			

McGraw-Hill Language Arts
Grade 4, Unit 4, Adjectives, pages 262–263

At Home: Use one sentence above as the beginning of a story. Tell your story to a family member.

▶ **Critical Thinking**

Name________________ Date__________ **Extend 53**

Articles: *a, an, the*

A. Write *a, an,* or *the* on the lines to complete the sayings or proverbs.

1. **An** apple a day keeps the doctor away.
2. **An** apple doesn't fall far from the tree.
3. **A** bad workman always blames his tools.
4. Beauty is in **the** eye of the beholder.
5. **The** best things come in small packages.
6. The bigger they are, **the** harder they fall.
7. Birds of **a** feather flock together.
8. You can't tell **a** book by its cover.
9. Feed **a** cold and starve **a** fever.
10. Let **the** buyer beware.
11. When **the** cat is away, **the** mice will play.
12. Every cloud has **a** silver lining.
13. Curiosity killed **the** cat.
14. **The or An** early bird catches the worm.
15. Early to bed and early to rise, makes **a** man healthy, wealthy, and wise.

B. Choose one proverb above and explain its meaning in your own words.

Answers will vary.

At Home: Ask a parent to share his or her favorite proverb with you. Then illustrate the proverb with a drawing.

McGraw-Hill Language Arts
Grade 4, Unit 4, Adjectives,
pages 264–265

▶ **Critical Thinking**

Name________________ Date__________ **Extend 54**

Adjectives After Linking Verbs

Pretend you were driving in the country and came across a farmer's vegetable stand. The farmer displayed signs to encourage you to buy his goods.

Read the signs. Circle the linking verbs. Underline the adjectives that describe the foods.

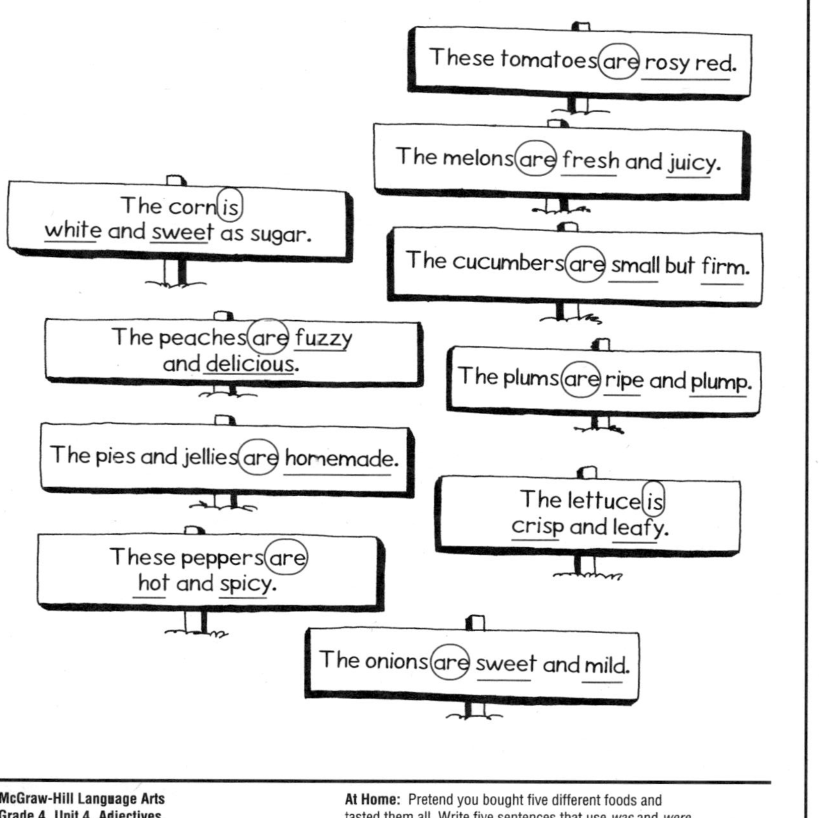

These tomatoes are rosy red.
The melons are fresh and juicy.
The corn is white and sweet as sugar.
The cucumbers are small but firm.
The peaches are fuzzy and delicious.
The plums are ripe and plump.
The pies and jellies are homemade.
The lettuce is crisp and leafy.
These peppers are hot and spicy.
The onions are sweet and mild.

McGraw-Hill Language Arts
Grade 4, Unit 4, Adjectives,
pages 266–267

At Home: Pretend you bought five different foods and tasted them all. Write five sentences that use *was* and *were* to describe what you ate.

▶ **Critical Thinking**

Name______________ Date__________ **Extend 55**

Mechanics and Usage: Proper Adjectives

Read each sentence and underline the proper adjective. Write it correctly on the line. Then color the flag appropriately.

1. The spanish flag has a red stripe on both the bottom and top of the flag. It has a wider yellow stripe or band in the center.
Spanish

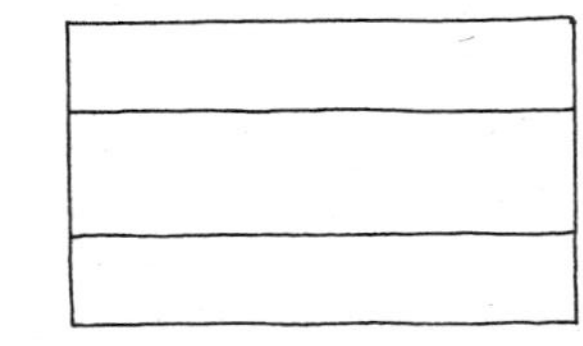

2. The turkish flag has a red background with a white crescent moon and a star in its center.
Turkish

3. The flag with a white background and a big red circle in the center belongs to the japanese. The circle stands for the rising sun.
Japanese

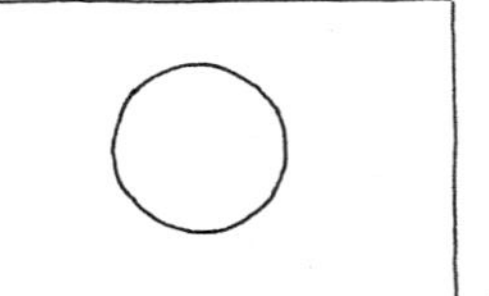

4. The french flag is divided lengthwise into three separate bands. From left to right it is blue, white, and red.
French

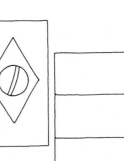

5. At the brazilian embassy, you would see this flag with its green background. In the center there is a blue globe on a yellow diamond. The center of the globe has a white line indicating the equator.
Brazilian

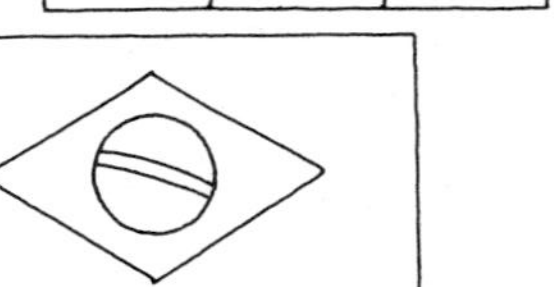

At Home: Design your own flag. Then write a description of it using a proper adjective.

▶ **Critical Thinking**

Name______________ Date__________ **Extend 56**

Mixed Review

Read all the sentences in each riddle. Then add the missing articles and adjectives. Finally, answer each riddle.

1. It has six legs.
It has a pair of wings.
It has three body parts.
It may hop, crawl, or fly.
What is it?
It's an insect.

2. It has scales.
It crawls on the ground.
It may be poisonous.
It is cold-blooded.
What is it?
It's a snake or reptile.

3. It has two wings.
It has very long skinny legs.
It is big but does not fly.
It sometimes puts its head in the sand.
It's an ostrich.

4. It is orange with black stripes.
It's a wild mammal that lives in Asia.
It purrs and growls.
It's a tiger.

At Home: Write up a riddle about a famous person, thing, or place to ask a family member. Try to include a proper adjective in your riddle.

▶ **Critical Thinking**

Name________________ Date________ **Extend 57**

Adjectives That Compare

Circle the adjective that compares in each sentence. Then, if you can, write the answer to the question on the line.

1. Which Wright brother was older, Wilbur or Orville? Wilbur
2. Which ocean is deeper, the Atlantic or the Pacific? Pacific
3. True or False: Mount Everest is the highest mountain in the world. True
4. Which lake is longer, Lake Michigan or Lake Superior? Superior
5. Is the Sears Tower in Chicago taller or shorter than the World Trade Center in New York? Taller
6. True or False: The world's longest river is the Amazon. True
7. True or False: Delaware is the smallest state in the U.S.A. False — Rhode Island
8. Is the highest U.S. mountain found in California or Alaska? Alaska — Mount McKinley
9. True or False: The cheetah is the fastest land animal. True
10. True or False: Plains are lower than the land around them. True
11. True or False: The oldest Moon rock brought back by the Apollo astronauts is about 4.6 billion years old. True
12. Which planet is closest to the sun? Mercury
13. Which planet is the largest? Jupiter
14. Which planet is closer to the sun, Earth or Pluto? Earth

At Home: Compare five facts about your state with five facts of a neighboring state.

▶ **Critical Thinking**

Name________________ Date________ **Extend 58**

Spelling Adjectives That Compare

A. Complete the chart by adding adjectives that compare. Watch the spelling!

Adjective	Compares Two Nouns	Compares Three or More Nouns
big	bigger	biggest
brave	braver	bravest
early	earlier	earliest
funny	funnier	funniest
gloomy	gloomier	gloomiest
happy	happier	happiest
hot	hotter	hottest
sad	sadder	saddest
sorry	sorrier	sorriest
wise	wiser	wisest

B. Write five sentences using words from the last two columns of the chart.

Sentences will vary.

At Home: Write three sentences that compare things in your home. For example: *The mat at the front door is larger than the one at the back door.*

▶ **Critical Thinking**

Name ________________ Date ________ **Extend 59**

Comparing with *More* and *Most*

The Little League playoffs are on! Here are the scoreboards for two different games. Read the questions below and answer each one in a complete sentence, using *more* or *most*.

Inning	1	2	3	4	5	6
Tigers	0	2	1	3	0	3
Lions	2	0	2	5	3	1

Inning	1	2	3	4	5	6
Sharks	4	1	0	3	2	4
Whales	2	1	3	3	2	4

1. Which team had the most impressive first inning?
The Sharks had the most impressive first inning.

2. Which of the two games was more exciting, and why?
The Sharks vs. Whales game was more exciting because the score was closer.

3. Which team faced the most difficult challenge in the sixth inning, and why?
The Tigers faced the most difficult challenge because they had to score more runs.

4. Which team had a more upsetting loss than the Sharks?
The Tigers had a more upsetting loss than the Sharks.

At Home: What do you like about baseball? Write a short paragraph. Use *more* and *most* when you can.

▶ **Critical Thinking**

Name ________________ Date ________ **Extend 60**

Comparing with *Good* and *Bad*

A. Use *good, better,* and *best* in each of the following sentences.

1. On the baseball field, I am **good** at catching fly balls, but Jim is **better** than I at fielding grounders, and Sarah is the **best** catcher ever.
2. In the music room, Jim is the **best** trumpet player in his age group, and Sarah is **better** than I at the piano; I am simply **good** but not great.
3. In art class, Sarah's paintings are **good**, but mine are **better** than hers, and Jim's are **best** of all.
4. In science class, Jim's projects are usually **good**, Sarah's are **better** than his and mine are always the **best** in the class.

B. Use *bad, worse,* and *worst* in each of the following sentences.

5. I have to admit I am **bad** at writing letters, and Sarah is **worse** than I, but the **worst** letter writer of all is Jim.
6. Jim is also **bad** at returning phone calls; I'm just a bit **worse**, but Sarah is **worst** of all three of us.
7. All three of us are **bad** at cleaning up our cubbies, but I think Sarah is the **worst** of us three, and mine always looks **worse** than Jim's.
8. In gym class I am **bad** on the swings, but Jim is **worse** than I, and Sarah is **worst** of all!

At Home: Write about a skill you do well and a skill you want to improve. How will you go about it?

▶ **Critical Thinking**

Name__________________ Date________ **Extend 61**

Combining Sentences: Adjectives

Pretend you wrote the following "draft" as a report for school. Now it's time to improve your writing. Rewrite the paragraph below. Combine sentences by moving an adjective from one sentence to another. **Answers will vary.**

A Day at a Museum

Mom took me to a museum yesterday. It was a natural history museum. We saw many dinosaur skeletons. The skeletons were huge. We saw fossils of footprints. The footprints were enormous. We read signs. The signs were informative. The Mesozoic era includes three periods. They are the Cretaceous, the Jurassic, and the Triassic.

I read about the *Allosaurus. Allosaurus* means "other lizard." It had a big body. It was 35 feet long. It had many teeth. Its teeth were sharp. Of course, it had a big jaw. Its jaw was powerful. It was a meat eater. It had two small forelegs. Each foreleg had three claws. The claws served as meat hooks. The claws were curved.

A Day at a Museum

Mom took me to a natural history museum yesterday. We saw many huge dinosaur skeletons. We saw fossils of enormous footprints. We read informative signs. The Mesozoic era includes the Cretaceous, the Jurassic, and the Triassic periods.

I read about the *Allosaurus*, which means "other lizard." Its big body was 35 feet long. It had many sharp teeth. Of course, it had a big, powerful jaw. It was a meat eater. It had two small forelegs, each with three claws. The curved claws served as meat hooks.

At Home: Create new names for other dinosaurs you know about and describe them in a paragraph.

▶ **Critical Thinking**

Name__________________ Date________ **Extend 62**

Mechanics and Usage: Letter Punctuation

Add the correct punctuation and capital letters to Jillian's letter. Then pretend you are Josephine and answer the letter. Use your own address in the letter you write.

october 7 2003 **October 7, 2003**
57 east fairware st **57 East Fairware St.**
Park city, utah 84060 **Park City, Utah 84060**
dear josephine **Dear Josephine,**

I can't believe it. I read in today's paper that ordinary people will be able to visit the moon soon. I have mixed feelings about going. Traveling in space just has to be a wonderful feeling. But I think I would be lonely for my friends if I stayed away for a long time. I would miss my parents and, yes, even my little brother.

Write to me and tell me what you think.

love jillian **Love, Jillian**

Letters will vary. Check students' punctuation.

At Home: Explain the advantages and disadvantages of living in a big city in a letter to a friend. Mail your letter or share it with a family member.

▶ **Critical Thinking**

Name_______________ Date_______ **Extend 63**

Mixed Review

A. Complete the sentences with the correct comparative adjectives.
Answers may vary. Possible answers are given.

1. The blue whale is the **largest/biggest** mammal in the world.
2. An elephant is **smaller** than a whale but **larger** than a hippopotamus.
3. The **longest** nose belongs to the African elephant.
4. The ostrich has a **longer** neck than the flamingo.
5. A tortoise is **more interesting** to watch than a slug.
6. The peacock has the **most beautiful** tail feathers of any other bird.
7. The Egyptian goose is the **highest** flier of all birds.
8. The **worst** zoo I have ever seen had small, dirty cages.
9. A zoo with a lot of wide open spaces is **better** than one with only tiny cages.
10. One of the **best** zoos in the world is in San Diego, California.

B. Underline the proper adjectives in the sentences above.

C. Combine the following sentences by adding an adjective to one sentence.

11. The giant anteater's tail is very long. The giant anteater's tail is sticky.
The giant anteater's tail is very long and sticky.
12. The Nile River alligator has a large jaw with many teeth. The Nile River alligator has sharp teeth.
The Nile River alligator has a large jaw with many sharp teeth.

At Home: Make up a fact book about people or animals. Use comparative adjectives in your book. Share your work with a family member.
▶ **Critical Thinking**

McGraw-Hill Language Arts
Grade 4, Unit 4, Mixed Review,
pages 284–285

Name_______________ Date_______ **Extend 64**

Common Errors: Adjectives

A. Read the story and underline the incorrect comparative adjectives. Write the correct adjectives on the lines below.

Clara's grandparents run Gardini's, one of the most popularest restaurants in town. It is the most hardest place to get a reservation. Other restaurants are much more fancier. Gardini's is most best for families and for people who like food made with the most freshest ingredients. Clara helps out during the most busiest times. Grandfather is the most nicest person, and he never loses his temper, even when the most worst catastrophes happen in the kitchen! Grandmother is demandinger, but she works in the kitchen and helps wait on tables, too, so her job is hecticer than Grandfather's. Grandfather and Grandmother agree that Clara is the most quickest table-setter there is. Sometimes Grandmother tells her to be more carefuller, but Clara has never broken a dish. When the restaurant is quiet, Clara fixes herself the most biggest bowl of soup and sits down to the most wonderfullest meal anywhere. Her grandparents are importanter to her than anyone else.

1. **most popular**	6. **busiest**	11. **quickest**
2. **hardest**	7. **nicest**	12. **more careful**
3. **fancier**	8. **worst**	13. **biggest**
4. **best**	9. **more demanding**	14. **most wonderful**
5. **freshest**	10. **more hectic**	15. **more important**

B. What is your favorite restaurant? Write about the last time your family ate out. Use comparative adjectives to describe your meal.

Answers will vary.

McGraw-Hill Language Arts
Grade 4, Unit 4, Adjectives,
pages 286–287

At Home: Write about your grandparents or another relative. Tell why that person is special to you. Use adjectives that compare.
▶ **Critical Thinking**

Name______________________ Date__________ **Extend 65**

Study Skills: Maps

Bei is studying United States history. She studied this map showing the settlers' original thirteen colonies and the areas settled by 1820 and by 1850.

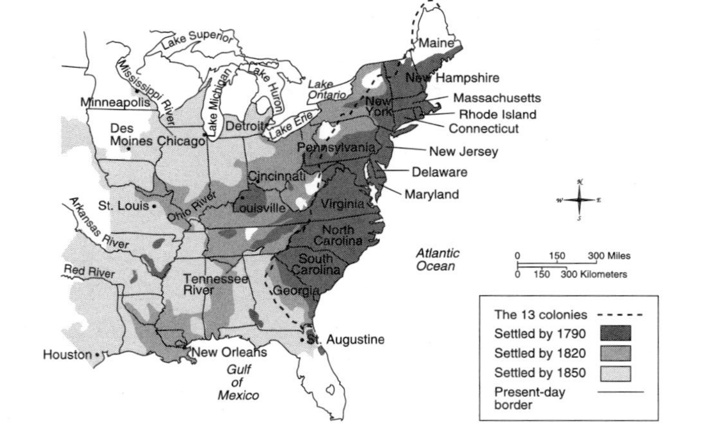

Use the information on the map to complete the sentences below.

1. In 1820, two modern-day cities north of St. Louis that were not yet settled were **Des Moines, Chicago** and **Minneapolis, Detroit**.
2. The **Atlantic Ocean** is the body of water to the east of the thirteen colonies.
3. By 1820, the southernmost city that was settled was **New Orleans**.
4. By 1850, the cities of **Houston** and **St. Augustine** were settled. They were as far south as the southernmost settled city in 1820.
5. The **Ohio** River had two settled cities on its banks by 1820. By 1850, more land was settled to the west and south of it.

At Home: Make some comparisons between settlements in 1850 and the United States today.

▶ **Critical Thinking**

Name______________________ Date__________ **Extend 66**

Vocabulary: Synonyms and Antonyms

Find a synonym or antonym for each word in the word search puzzle below. Look for words across, down, and diagonally. Circle the word in the puzzle, then write it on the correct line.

Synonyms

neat	**tidy**	recreation	**fun**
error	**mistake**	ask	**question**
glisten	**shine**	choose	**select**

Antonyms

before	**after**	worry	**calm**
beautiful	**homely**	more	**less**
sunrise	**dusk**	ruin	**repair**

```
V U M C B T O F I
C D S E R I O U S
U T R F R D Y N E
H O M E L Y T X L
D S I M P E A S E
U H S N O A S W C
S I T X C Z I S T
K N A F T E R R D
R E K C A L M B O
Q U E S T I O N N
```

At Home: Create a crossword puzzle using the above words.

▶ **Critical Thinking**

Name______________________ Date__________ **Extend 67**

Composition: Organization

A. Find the time-order words and spatial words in the paragraph below and write them in the chart.

When I first came to Wildwood School, I didn't know anyone. I sat beside a girl named Wendy. Wendy sat next to a boy named Fred. As soon as I sat down, Wendy and Fred asked me my name and where I was from. Then they introduced me to a few more kids in the class. When the teacher came in, she had me stand up in front of the group. I had to give a little speech about myself and then go over to the map and show the class my hometown. Later I went to lunch with Fred and another boy named Carlo. His grandmother lives near the city I used to live in, and he visited her there a long time ago. After lunch we played outside. Wendy and Carlo and I climbed on top of the play structure, and we played wall ball. Ever since that day, Wendy and Carlo and Fred have been my good friends, and I feel lucky that I moved to such a nice place!

Time-order Words	Spatial Words
first	beside
As soon as	next to
Then	in front of
When the teacher came in	over
then	near
Later	outside
a long time ago	on top of
After	
Ever since	

B. What is it like to be the new kid in a situation? On another sheet of paper, use time-order words and spatial words to tell about how you have made new friends. **Answers will vary. Check to make sure students use time-order and spatial words.**

At Home: Discuss with a family member how time-order words and spatial words help you to organize your writing.

▶ **Critical Thinking**

Name______________________ Date__________ **Extend 68**

Pronouns

Look at the picture. Then add a pronoun that completes each sentence.

1. **It** is spring because the trees are budding.
2. The girl who is jumping has a bow in **her** hair.
3. **She** is a very good jumper!
4. The girls who are turning the rope have **their** left hands at **their** sides.
5. **They** look like they are having a lot of fun.
6. The dog looks like **it** wants to jump, too.
7. It seems that the boy has **its** leash.
8. **He** must have forgotten to put the leash on the dog.
9. "**I** have to take you home now," said the boy.
10. "**We** are going to the vet in just a little while."

At Home: Explain possible mishaps that can occur when a dog is left off its leash.

▶ **Critical Thinking**

Name ______________ Date ________ **Extend 69**

Subject Pronouns

Circle all the subject pronouns in the following jokes.

I love to
tell riddles and jokes.
You will like these:

"We serve anything the customer wants," said a restaurant sign. So I went in and ordered roasted rocket ship and fries. The waiter said, "Certainly, sir." He went into the kitchen. He returned looking sad. "I bet you have no rocket ship," said another customer with a smirk.

"It is not that, sir," answered the waiter. "We have no potatoes."

We asked the waiter, "What's on the menu today?"

He answered, "Everything."

I said, "Bring us everything, then."

He shouted to the cook, "Two orders of hash!"

She asked the waiter, "Will the pancakes be long?"

"No, Madam, they will be round, as usual."

At Home: Create a menu for a silly restaurant. Describe each item. Circle any subject pronouns on your menu.

▶ **Critical Thinking**

Name ______________ Date ________ **Extend 70**

Object Pronouns

Underline the object pronoun in each sentence.

At the Nature Center

Come with me to the wildlife preserve. I will introduce you to Mrs. Whitcomb. She will explain to us how beavers build their ponds. We will be able to see them busy at work.

Mrs. Whitcomb brought along her teenage son, Derek, who helps her. He said he'd take us on a nature walk. I showed him my gold bird feather. He liked it and said we'd look for a bird that had gold feathers.

We saw chipmunk holes and saw two critters scurry down into them. We heard a rat-a-tat-tat, rat-a-tat-tat not too far from us.

"Derek," I asked pointing to a woodpecker up in a tree, "Did my feather come from it?"

"Yes," said Derek, "it looks like a yellow-shafted flicker to me."

At Home: Describe a bird that lives in your neighborhood. Use object pronouns. Then draw a picture of it. Show your work to a family member.

▶ **Critical Thinking**

Name______________________ Date__________ **Extend 71**

Mechanics and Usage: Punctuation in Dialogue

Pretend you interviewed people for a newspaper story. Below are your notes. Rewrite them as a story for your school paper. Add paragraphs, quotation marks, and other punctuation where needed.

I asked students what they thought of the new after-school program. Jill said I like it because I finish my paintings in the art room. I don't like it said Ali. My parents insist I come, but I would rather play ball with my friends in the park. June said I like it because my mom can't pick me up until 6:00. Later I went to speak to Ms. Freemont who runs the program. She said I think this program has been needed for a long time. I also spoke to Mr. Quimbley, our principal. He said we are lucky that the mayor has given us money for the program. It's going to be the best in the city.

I asked students what they thought of the new after-school program.

Jill said, "I like it because I finish my paintings in the art room."

"I don't like it," said Ali. "My parents insist I come, but I would rather play ball with my friends in the park."

June said, "I like it because my mom can't pick me up until 6:00."

Later I went to speak to Ms. Freemont who runs the program. She said, "I think this program has been needed for a long time."

I also spoke to Mr. Quimbley, our principal. He said, "We are lucky that the mayor has given us money for the program. It's going to be the best in the city."

At Home: Discuss a current event with a parent. Express your views about it.

Name______________________ Date__________ **Extend 72**

Mixed Review

A. On the line, write *subject* if the underlined pronoun is a subject pronoun. Write *object* if it is an object pronoun.

1. I like to read folk tales and trickster tales. **subject**
2. They are fun to read aloud. **subject**
3. My younger sister likes me to read them to her. **object**
4. Then she retells them to me in her own words. **object**
5. Sometimes my Dad reads trickster tales to both of us. **object**

B. Underline only the subject and object pronouns in the following tale. Add a title and an ending to the story. Use more subject and object pronouns.
Titles and endings will vary.

One day a small terrier named Spot stole a large steak from a woman's shopping bag. She chased him, but she couldn't catch him. Spot ran with the steak into the woods. On his way, he came to a stream. He looked into the water and saw a dog with a steak in his mouth. Spot jumped into the water to grab the steak from him. And while jumping, he also gave out a loud bark.

Spot no longer saw the other dog or his steak. Spot hungrily watched as the steak was carried away with the current.

At Home: Write a simple fable or tale. Use subject and object pronouns. Share your tale with a family member.

McGraw-Hill School Division

Name ______ Date ______ **Extend 73**

Pronoun-Verb Agreement

Choose a verb from the word box to complete each sentence. Write the correct form of the verb. Then write the name of the person or thing that the subject pronoun refers to. **Answers will vary.**

eat	feed	fight	go	live	list
reach	speed	spin	vote	wear	write

1. She **fights** fires. **firefighter**
2. It **speeds** to a burning building. **firetruck**
3. Together they **fight** the flames. **firefighters**
4. They **reach** the leaves of trees with their long necks. **giraffes**
5. It **spins** a chrysalis and changes into an insect that flies. **caterpillar**
6. He **feeds** and cares for the gorillas. **zookeeper**
7. He **lives** in the White House. **President of the U.S.A.**
8. They **write** laws for our country. **Representatives and Senators**
9. We **vote** for our lawmakers. **citizens**
10. We **eat** there when we don't want to stay home and cook. **people/Mom and I**
11. He **wears** a hat when he prepares food. **chef**
12. It **lists** the specials of the day. **menu**

At Home: Create five more sentences like those above. Read them to family members and ask who or what the subject refers to.

▶ **Critical Thinking**

Name ______ Date ______ **Extend 74**

Combining Sentences

Combine the sentences by joining two or more pronouns in the subject or the predicate. You may want to replace two singular pronouns with a plural pronoun. **Answers may vary.**

1. You have a book on volcanoes. He has a book on volcanoes.
You and he have books on volcanoes. / They have books...
2. I will place the books on the shelf. She will place the books on the shelf.
She and I will place the books on the shelves. / We will...
3. He works the computer. You work the computer.
He and you work the computer. / They will...
4. She helped her get on-line. I helped her get on-line.
She and I helped her get on-line. / We helped her get on-line.
5. Sophie thanked me. Sophie thanked her.
Sophie thanked her and me. / Sophie thanked us.
6. Mrs. Reasoner said he and she talk too much. Mrs. Reasoner said I talk too much, too.
Mrs. Reasoner said that he, she, and I talk too much. / ...we talk...
7. You can find pictures in that file next to him. You can find pictures in that file next to me.
You can find pictures in that file next to me and him. / us.
8. Phillipa dropped a stack of books near him. I dropped a stack of books near her.
Phillipa and I dropped a stack of books near him and her. / them.
9. "Too much noise," she said "Too much noise," he said.
"Too much noise," he and she said. / "Too much noise," they said.
10. Will you walk her home? Will you walk me home?
Will you walk her and me home? / Will you walk us home?

At Home: Discuss ideas for a neighborhood book swap.

▶ **Critical Thinking**

Name ______ Date ______ **Extend 75**

Possessive Pronouns

Complete the sentences by adding possessive pronouns. **Some answers may vary. Possible answers are given.**

__**My/Our**__ parents are planning a family vacation. Mom wants to visit __**her**__ mother in Seattle. Dad wants to use __**his**__ new camping gear somewhere in the mountains. __**My**__ sister and I told them we wanted to stay home and play with __**our**__ new friends who just moved in across the street. __**Their**__ new puppy is adorable, and we all like to play with it. Its ears flop around __**its**__ eyes. We were just kidding, but __**my/our**__ parents, didn't realize it.

"Why can't we make everyone happy?" __**my/our**__ father asked Mom. "You can visit __**your**__ mother. Then you and I will go camping with __**my**__ new gear, and the kids can stay home with a babysitter."

"__**Your**__ idea is not a good one," I said.

"We have changed __**our**__ minds," said __**my**__ sister.

"Oh," said Dad, "I bet you want to go to __**your**__ favorite amusement park."

"__**Your**__ hunch is right," I said. "We really want to visit Grandmother, go camping with you, and go to an amusement park, too."

"That settles that," said Dad. "Now everyone is happy."

At Home: Write about a vacation you would enjoy with your family. Use possessive pronouns.

Name ______ Date ______ **Extend 76**

Mechanics and Usage: Contractions, Pronouns and Verbs

Enjoy the jokes. Then change a pronoun and a verb to a contraction to make the writing smoother.

Teacher: Peter, name two pronouns.
Peter: Who, me?
Teacher: You are right! __**You're**__

Tim: If I gave you three gerbils this afternoon and three tomorrow, how many would you have?
Peter: Eight. I have got two already. __**I've**__

Dad: Peter, you have got your shoes on the wrong feet. __**you've**__
Peter: They are the only feet I have. __**They're**__

Teacher: Get out your chemistry book. We are going to study nitrates. Peter, tell us what you know about nitrates. __**We're**__
Peter: Mom says they are usually twice the day rates. __**they're**__

Mom: Peter, I wish you would pay a little more attention. __**you'd**__
Peter: I am paying as little attention as possible. __**I'm**__

Peter: I have just had a brilliant idea. __**I've**__
Lee: It is probably beginner's luck. __**It's**__

At Home: Write a joke or riddle about a child and a parent. Share it with a family member.

Name______________________ Date__________ **Extend 77**

Mixed Review

A. Add a present, past, or future-tense verb to each sentence as indicated in the parentheses. Make sure the verb agrees with the subject pronoun. **Answers will vary. Samples are shown.**

1. He (present) **likes/wants** to make the masks for our school play.
2. She (past) **finished/completed** the last of the script writing.
3. They (future) **will work** on the scenery tomorrow.
4. It (past) **fell/crashed** to the ground yesterday.
5. We all (past) **picked** it up and made it stand again.

B. Combine the following sentences. **Answers will vary. Samples are shown.**

6. Are you in the play? Is he in the play?
   Are you and he in the play?
7. I asked him to be a talking tree. I asked her to be a talking tree.
   I asked him or her to be a talking tree.
8. He turned down the part. She turned down the part.
   They turned down the part. (or) He and she turned down the part.
9. She said she wanted to work the lights. He said he wanted to work the lights.
   They said they wanted to work the lights.
10. They were getting frustrated. I was getting frustrated.
    We were getting frustrated.

C. Write a sentence that includes the possessive pronoun in parentheses. Will you use it in the subject or the predicate? Try to stick with the "class play" theme. **Sentences will vary.**

11. (my) ______________________
12. (your) ______________________

At Home: Write some dialogue for a skit. Use subject, object, and possessive pronouns. Read your dialogue out loud with a family member. Each of you read a part.

▶ **Critical Thinking**

Name______________________ Date__________ **Extend 78**

Common Errors: Pronouns

Marcy made the following speech at the school assembly, telling about an honor that she and her classmates received. Choose the correct pronouns and write them on the lines to finish the sentences in the speech.

The students in Mrs. Rey's class are happy to announce that **we** have been chosen to represent Hill School at the City Art Show. The show will be held the third weekend in April, and **its** purpose is to raise money for the people of Carter County. As **you** know, many of **them** lost their homes in the recent flood. **We** want to do everything **we** can to help. The mural that **our** class designed will be hanging in the lobby at City Hall. The mural is over 12 feet long, and **it** shows the city skyline. The mayor, who was one of the judges, said **he** had never seen such a wonderful collage. **We** used a variety of things to create **our** masterpiece. **It** is very colorful and busy, and **you** will see that lots of familiar city sights have been included in the scene. Mrs. Andrews said that **she** will take a group to the show on Saturday morning. **I** urge **you** to try and come along. **It** will be a fun trip, and **it** is for a good cause. If **you** have any questions, don't hesitate to contact **me** or someone else in Mrs. Rey's class.

At Home: What kind of money-raising projects are going on in your community? Write up an announcement for a cause that interests you. Be sure to use pronouns correctly.

▶ **Critical Thinking**

Name______________________ Date__________ **Extend 79**

Study Skills: Dictionary

Tori read an editorial in her school newspaper. She was unsure of the meanings of some of the words, so she used information from the dictionary to create her own personal dictionary.

Use Tori's personal dictionary and write the part of speech and meaning for each underlined word in the editorial.

A perfect complement to a school day is a late afternoon full of fun activities. It is a principal concern of teachers and parents that students find clubs or teams they can enjoy. Some students believe it is a capital idea to join a club, like the drama club. Others choose another course of action—that is, a sports team. Teachers are happy to counsel students about their choices. We encourage everyone to try out some new activities but not desert their favorites.

1. complement **noun; something that completes or makes perfect**
2. principal **adjective; most important**
3. capital **adjective; excellent**
4. course **noun; path of action**
5. counsel **verb; to give advice**
6. desert **verb; to leave**

capital (kaɔ´ i təl) *adj.* **1.** most important **2.** where government is located **3.** excellent; very fine **4.** that which is punished by death *n.* **1.** upper case letter **2.** place where government is located **3.** money or property **4.** the top part of a column

complement (kom´ plə mənt) *n.* **1.** something that completes or makes perfect **2.** the full number needed **3.** the word(s) that complete a predicate *v.* to make complete or perfect by supplying what is needed.

counsel (koun´ səl) *n.* **1.** advice or opinion **2.** exchanging ideas by talking together **3.** lawyer(s) who handle a case *v.* **1.** to give advice **2.** to urge or recommend

course (kôrs) *n.* **1.** path of action **2.** a choice that continues over time **3.** a direction taken **4.** a way of acting **5.** like things in an order **6.** part of a meal **7.** a single or complete series of studies in a subject *v.* to run or race through

desert (di zûrt´) *v.* **1.** to leave **2.** to abandon a military position or post without permission *n.* (de´ zûrt) **1.** a dry, sandy region **2.** wild and not lived in

principal (prin´ sə pəl) *adj.* **1.** most important *n.* **1.** a person or thing of first importance **2.** the head of a school **3.** sum of money invested or owed, not counting interest.

At Home: Select a word from the editorial and a meaning other than the one used in the editorial. Write a sentence showing how it is used.

▶ **Critical Thinking**

Name______________________ Date__________ **Extend 80**

Vocabulary: Homophones and Homographs

Complete the puzzle by writing the correct homophone or homograph.

Across

1. Part of a tree
3. Past tense of *eat*
5. A ______________ of shoes
6. A peck on the cheek
8. It cost 5 ______________.
10. When you cry, ______________ flow from your eyes.
11. "When the ______________ blows, the cradle will rock."

Down

1. If you ______________ a vase, it will shatter into many pieces.
2. A kind of rabbit
4. It follows seven.
7. Part of a play
9. You go up and down these.

1 b	r	a	n	c	2 h				
r					3 a	t	4 e		
e		5 p	a	i	r		i		
a					e		g		
6 k	i	7 s	s				h		
		c					t		
	8 c	e	n	t	9 s				
		n			10 t	e	a	r	s
		e			a				
				11 w	i	n	d		
					r				
					s				

At Home: Use the answers from the puzzle to write a few pairs of homophones. For example, a homophone pair for 2 Down is *hair-hare.*

▶ **Critical Thinking**

Name__________ Date______ Extend 81

Composition: Writing Dialogue

Read the dialogue examples below. Then answer the questions.

"I told Ed that the bus would be late," said Bill, "so he got a ride with Jess."

1. Who is the speaker? Bill

"Glen is in my class," said Hattie. "He seems nice." "He is nice," said Lisa. "I sat with him last year."

2. Who is having this dialogue? Hattie and Lisa
3. What should be done to correct this dialogue?
"He is nice" should be indented on a new line.

"Do you have a new bike, Kim? asked Lucy.
"No, I just cleaned up my old one!" said Kim.

4. Who is asking the question? Lucy
5. What should be done to correct this dialogue?
Put quotation marks after the question mark.

"Do you have the homework assignment?" asked Bruno.
"I don't have it, said Ben, but I think Carly does."

6. Name the person Bruno is talking to. Ben
7. What should be done to correct this dialogue?
Put quotation marks after the first comma and after the second comma.

"could you pick up a quart of milk for me?" asked Mom.
"Sure," said Tom. "I'll bring it home after school.

8. Name the person Tom is talking to. Mom
9. What should be done to correct this dialogue?
Capitalize the *C* in *could* and put quotation marks after the period that follows the word *school*.

At Home: Whom do you like to talk to? Call a friend, and then jot down your conversation. Be sure to punctuate your dialogue correctly.

▶ **Critical Thinking**

Name__________ Date______ Extend 82

Adverbs That Tell *How*

A. Underline the adverb in each tongue twister. Then circle the verb that the adverb describes.

1. Fred frantically (flees) fifty-five flying fireflies.
2. Peter Piper prudently (picked) pitted plums.
3. Wally Williams wildly (whacks) whiffle balls.
4. Speedily, Suzie Smith (sprints).
5. Dennis (digs) diligently in the dusty den.
6. Presley (picked) a pound of prickly pears perfectly.
7. Señor Sanchez swiftly (sheared) sixty-seven sheep.
8. Sandy's son suddenly (shines) several scuffed shoes.
9. Theo fearlessly (threw) three free throws.
10. Sarah sees the setting sun (sink) swiftly.

B. Make up two tongue twisters that include adverbs.

11. Answers will vary.

12. __________

At Home: Take the challenge. Write one silly sentence with as many adverbs in it as you can.

▶ **Critical Thinking**

Name________________ Date__________ **Extend 83**

Adverbs That Tell *When* or *Where*

A man sitting on a sidewalk bench on Main Street saw an accident happen in the middle of the street. A police officer asked him to write a report of what he saw. Here is what he wrote.

Underline all the adverbs that tell where or when. Then write them on the lines below.

The accident happened today right here in the middle of Main Street. I was outside waiting for a friend. I was early. The accident happened suddenly on Main Street. The taxi was parked near the curb. It quickly pulled out and rammed the convertible's back right fender. The woman stood in front of her convertible and called 911 on her cell phone. Then she drove her car to the side of the road. The taxi driver remained in his taxi. Finally, the police arrived.

today	here	outside	early
suddenly	near	quickly	front
Then	finally		

At Home: Write detailed directions on how to get from your home to a relative's house.

▶ **Critical Thinking**

Name________________ Date__________ **Extend 84**

Adverbs That Compare

Add *-er* or *-est* to each adverb in parentheses. Write the word on the line to make the sentence read correctly.

My Puppy

It's been (hard) **harder** to convince my mom than my dad to get me a puppy. Mom first said that the (early) **earliest** I can get one is next spring. That was (long) **longer** than I had expected to wait. I promised to walk, feed, and brush the dog every day.

Finally, Mom answered in her (strong) **strongest** voice ever, "Okay, I give in. You'll get your puppy (soon) **sooner** than next spring."

Dad said that we could visit an animal shelter that is (near) **nearer** to his office than to my Mom's. The (early) **earliest** Dad said he could take me was next Saturday. The (close) **closer** Saturday came, the more excited I got.

I now have the cutest puppy you can imagine. It barks (loud) **louder** in the evening than it does in the daytime. It jumps (high) **higher** than my knees. Best of all, it sleeps and snores softly in my room every night.

At Home: What kind of pet would you suggest to a friend? Write instructions for someone on how to care for that pet.

▶ **Critical Thinking**

Name ____________ Date ________ **Extend 85**

More Adverbs That Compare

Add *more* or *most* to complete each sentence.

1. Jody waited the **most** anxiously of anyone in class.
2. Troy learned his lines **more** slowly than Phil.
3. Jody recited her lines **most** eloquently of all.
4. The scene that takes place in Bali passed the **most** swiftly of all the scenes.
5. The males danced **more** rhythmically than the females.
6. We rehearsed **more** determinedly today than yesterday.
7. Ramon painted **more** frantically than Jordon to finish the scenery on time.
8. He drew the trees **more** quickly than he did the bushes.
9. Our auditorium can seat guests **more** comfortably than our cafeteria.
10. My parents cheer and applaud **most** loudly of all the parents.

At Home: Use *more* and *most* to compare the outdoor activities that you and your family engage in.

Name ____________ Date ________ **Extend 86**

Mechanics and Usage: *Good* and *Well*

Add *good* or *well* to complete each sentence.

"It's always a **good** idea to maintain **good** health habits," said Ms. Taylor, our school nurse. "If you want to keep healthy and **well**, you have to eat good foods. You also must do a **good** amount of physical exercise every day."

"Who can demonstrate some **good** exercises?" she asked.

Belinda offered to show us how to do push-ups. She did them quite **well**. Ms. Taylor said, "**Good** job, Belinda!"

Then Ms. Taylor asked us to list **good** healthful foods that are part of the food pyramid. Anna writes **well**, so she listed the foods on the chalkboard, and we copied them in our notebooks.

Then it was time to be weighed and measured, so we went to Ms. Taylor's office. "You have gained only a pound since the fall, and that's **good** for your height," Ms. Taylor told Amy.

"Oh, dear, you don't look **well**," said Ms. Taylor, looking at Joseph's eyes. She checked his forehead to see if he had a fever. "I think it would be **good** if you went home now. I am sure you will get **well**

At Home: Make a poster that shows how to keep safe in your home. Show it to a family member.

Name__________ Date________ **Extend 87**

Mixed Review

A. Underline the adverb in each sentence. Then on the line, write *how, where,* or *when* to tell what question the adverb answers.

1. He ran quietly through the house. **how**
2. He ran up against the tabby yesterday. **when**
3. That feline was extremely fast. **how**
4. He stayed close to the entrance. **where**
5. He knew that cat stayed around. **where**

B. Write an adverb that compares the actions. **Answers may vary. Samples are given.**

6. This frog leaped **higher** than the one over there.
7. Grandma screamed the **loudest** when one frog jumped into the punch bowl.
8. We kids scurried **faster** than the grownups, as we tried to catch them.
9. The dog barked **longer** than I had ever heard him bark before.
10. We all laughed **harder** than ever before!

C. Create a crossword puzzle or a word search puzzle which includes adverbs on this page. Run off copies of your puzzle and share it with classmates.

At Home: Use *good* and *well* in two separate sentences. Share your sentences with family members.

▶ **Critical Thinking**

Name__________ Date________ **Extend 88**

Negatives

Baby Talk

Sometimes when learning to talk, toddlers use more than one negative in a sentence. Rewrite each of the following sentences so that each one has only one negative word. **Answers will vary. Possible answers are given.**

1. I don't never want to go to bed.
   I don't ever want to go to bed.
2. Nobody never plays with me.
   Nobody ever plays with me.
3. I can't find my socks nowhere.
   I can't find my socks anywhere.
4. I haven't no more cookies.
   I haven't any more cookies.
5. You aren't never going to find me!
   You will never find me!
6. I didn't do nothing!
   I didn't do anything!
7. She doesn't like me no more.
   She doesn't like me anymore.
8. No one can find my puzzle pieces nowhere.
   No one can find my puzzle pieces anywhere.
9. They can't do none of it.
   They can't do any of it.
10. I'm not no baby; I'm a big boy.
    I am not a baby; I am a big boy.

At Home: Write a paragraph about something humorous a young child might say or do. Check the paragraph for two negatives in one sentence.

▶ **Critical Thinking**

Name____________________ Date__________ **Extend 89**

Prepositions

Unscramble the sentences and write them on the lines. Then underline the preposition in each sentence. Three lines from well-known nursery rhymes are included. Find and circle them.

Scrambled Sentences

1. fence cat is the on the
   The cat is on the fence.
2. the treetop bird flew to the
   The bird flew to the treetop.
3. puppy ran under porch the the
   The puppy ran under the porch.
4. the clock ran mouse up the
   The mouse ran up the clock.
5. vegetable the garden far is tree from the apple
   The apple tree is far from the vegetable garden. The vegetable garden is far from the apple tree.
6. an old lived shoe there who was woman in a
   There was an old woman who lived in a shoe.
7. behind is the tree Jorge
   Jorge is behind the tree. The tree is behind Jorge.
8. cat the climb Jorge up tree the and
   The cat and Jorge climb up the tree. Jorge and the cat climb up the tree.
9. dish away with spoon the ran the
   The dish ran away with the spoon.
10. toward tree Paula running is the
    Paula is running toward the tree.

At Home: What was your favorite nursery rhyme when you were younger? Write it and circle any prepositions you find.

▶ **Critical Thinking**

Name____________________ Date__________ **Extend 90**

Prepositional Phrases

Read each story starter and underline the prepositional phrase in each one. Then write one sentence that will continue each story.

1. There was an old rabbit beneath an old oak tree.
2. Beyond the bridge three dragons protected the castle.
3. The young boy lost his way in the deep dark woods.
4. Out popped a young dinosaur from the picnic basket.
5. It was green from top to bottom.
6. The police were on patrol all night long.
7. The telephone was ringing off the hook.
8. Grandma told me this story while sitting on her porch swing.
9. The bear was right between us!
10. I jumped right into the swimming hole.

Students' sentences will vary.

At Home: Choose a story from above to complete. Write it or tell it to a family member.

▶ **Critical Thinking**

Name________________ Date__________ **Extend 91**

Combining Sentences: Complex Sentences

Use the conjunctions in the word box to combine each pair of sentences.
Answers will vary. Possible answers are given.

although	because	while	since	when	yet

1. I was digging in our backyard. I found an arrowhead.
   I was digging in our backyard when I found an arrowhead.
2. I asked my dad a lot of questions. He told me what he knew.
   Since I asked my dad a lot of questions, he told me what he knew.
3. Uncovering objects takes a long time. Archaeologists do not want to harm any treasures.
   Uncovering objects takes a long time because archaeologists do not want to harm any treasures.
4. Archaeologists have helped us learn about the past. There is still a lot more to learn.
   Although archaeologists have helped us learn about the past, there is still a lot more to learn.
5. Scientists want to know how old an object is. They test the carbon in an object.
   When scientists want to know how old an object is, they test its carbon.
6. Some pictures are painted on cave walls. Others are painted on rocks.
   Some pictures are painted on cave walls, while others are painted on rocks.

At Home: Explain the difference between an *archaeologist* and a *paleontologist*. Use conjunctions to combine some sentences in your explanation.

▶ **Critical Thinking**

Name________________ Date__________ **Extend 92**

Mechanics and Usage: Commas

Add commas where they belong. Read the skit aloud with a partner. Pause after a comma.

Jody: Liz,why didn't you come to chorus practice?

Liz: Well,Samantha,don't you remember I had my art class after school?

Jody: No,I forgot.

Liz: Mr. Lennard said I could miss one practice a week, Jody.

Jody: Yes,I remember now. That's because you always sing on key.

Liz: No,that's not really true, but I do learn the lyrics fast.

Jody: Well,I wish I could say the same.

Liz: You won't believe this,but Mr. Lennard said I wasn't ready to sing that solo.

Jody: No,really? I'll help you practice,Liz.

Liz: What a friend you are, Jody!

Jody: Liz,would you like to help me out?

Liz: Sure,Jody,just name it.

Jody: Grab a spoon,friend,and help me finish this banana split!

At Home: Add a narrator's part to the beginning and ending of the skit above. Use commas in the dialogue.

▶ **Critical Thinking**

Name________________ Date__________ **Extend 93**

Mixed Review

A. First, rewrite each sentence to correct the double negative. Then underline the prepositions in the sentences. **Sentences may vary.**

1. I never see no one I know at the movie theater.
   I never see anyone I know at the movie theatre.
2. If I call from here, she won't never believe me.
   If I call from here, she won't ever believe me.
3. Nobody never told me it was about a scary monster.
   I was never told it was about a scary monster.
4. Since the robot couldn't never help, I jumped under my seat.
   Since the robot couldn't help, I jumped under my seat.

B. Create complex sentences with the pairs of sentences. Then underline the prepositional phrases in each complex sentence.

5. On Wednesdays, I go to a pottery class. I work on the potter's wheel.
   On Wednesdays, I go to a pottery class, where I work on the potter's wheel.
6. I made a bowl for my mother. She likes what I make.
   I made a bowl for my mother because she likes what I make.
7. My teacher wants to exhibit the bowl in a show. She likes it very much.
   My teacher wants to exhibit the bowl in a show since she likes it very much.
8. I will start on a vase. I am finished glazing the bowl.
   I will start on a vase when I am finished glazing the bowl.

At Home: Write a letter to a friend. Use at least three complex sentences. Ask a family member to proof your letter before you mail it.
▶ **Critical Thinking**

Name________________ Date__________ **Extend 94**

Common Errors: Adverbs

A. Read the fable below. Correct any errors you find in how adverbs and double negatives have been used. Make corrections above the lines.

The Fox and the Grapes

Once upon a time there was a fox who could ~~not~~ never get enough grapes. Every day, he looked ~~careful~~ **carefully** and sniffed the air ~~deep~~ **deeply** to find grapes to eat. One day he stopped ~~sudden~~ **suddenly** in his tracks. Dangling ~~inviting~~ **invitingly** above his head was the most beautiful cluster of grapes he had ever seen!

"Oh boy!" he said ~~excited~~ **excitedly**. "I can't ~~not~~ wait to taste those grapes."

The fox stretched on his tiptoes until he thought he would ~~complete~~ **completely** come apart, but he couldn't ~~not~~ reach the grapes. He ran ~~swift~~ **swiftly** and leaped ~~graceful~~ **gracefully** into the air, but he still couldn't ~~not~~ reach the grapes.

"This is not good," he muttered ~~angry~~ **angrily**. "I will ~~not~~ never taste those grapes."

The fox ~~stubborn~~ **stubbornly** kept jumping and leaping and reaching. After trying over and over to snag those grapes, he was ~~final~~ **finally** forced to give up.

"I didn't ~~never~~ really want to eat those grapes anyway," he said. "I'm sure they were sour."

B. On a separate sheet of paper, write another ending for this fable. Use adverbs.

At Home: What myths, legends, fables, or fairy tales do you like? Rewrite a traditional story and share it with your family. Be sure to use adverbs correctly.
▶ **Critical Thinking**

Name________________ Date________ **Extend 95**

Study Skills: Encyclopedia

A. Elise and Adam are partners in a research contest. They must look up answers to questions to earn points that will win them first place.

Help them by circling the key word in each question. In which volume of the encyclopedia should they look to find the answers to the questions? Write the volume number in the box to the right of each question.

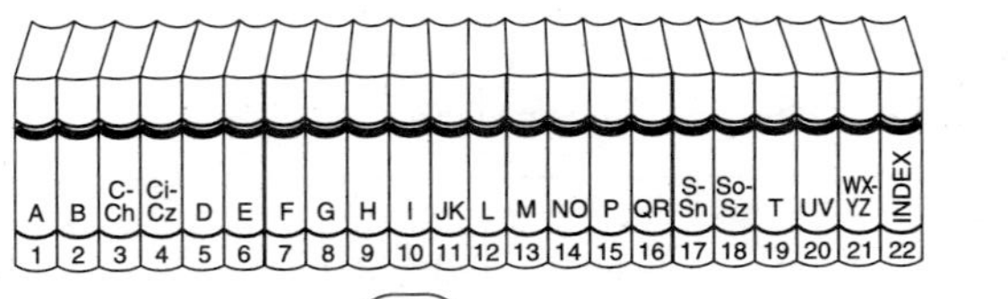

1. When did the painter Maurice Utrillo live? **20**
2. What is the climate of the country of Costa Rica? **4**
3. Who is Maya Angelou? **1**
4. Where is Canterbury located? **3**
5. Who was the father of King Frederick IV of Denmark and Norway? **7**
6. What do you find on the periodic table? **15**
7. Bactra was an ancient Greek kingdom. In what present-day country was Bactra located? **2**
8. What was Isamu Noguchi famous for? **14**
9. What are some traditions of the Hopi people? **9**

B. Write the volume numbers for the questions in the magic square to the right. If your answers are correct, the sum of all the rows, across and down, will be the same.

25

20 (1)	4 (2)	1 (3)
3 (4)	7 (5)	15 (6)
2 (7)	14 (8)	9 (9)

At Home: Make up a question that you can answer by looking up an entry in each volume of the encyclopedia.

▶ **Critical Thinking**

Name________________ Date________ **Extend 96**

Vocabulary: Suffixes

Below are definitions. Write the word that is being defined. Remember to add the correct suffix to each word.

1. washable: capable of being washed
2. painless: without pain
3. farmer: one who farms
4. dirty: having dirt
5. joyful: full of joy
6. miserable: in misery, capable of being miserable
7. slowly: in a slow manner
8. harmful: full of harm
9. thoughtless: without thought
10. completely: in a complete manner
11. excitement: result of being excited
12. miner: one who mines
13. brainless: without a brain
14. believable: capable of believing
15. shopper: one who shops

At Home: Include five words from above in a paragraph about someone's occupation.

▶ **Critical Thinking**

Name____________ Date________ **Extend 97**

Composition: Outlining

Use the words and phrases to fill in an outline for a report about your skeleton. Use the encyclopedia if you need help.

Your skeleton from head to toe		allows for different types of movement		
29 bones in face, head, jaws		6 bones for hearing		
26 bones in foot		femur and ulna	Arms and legs	
protects organs		supports your body	opposable thumb	
ribcage	Torso	vertebrae	hipbones	Skull

I. Your skeleton from head to toe
- **A.** supports your body
- **B.** protects organs
- **C.** allows for different types of movement

II. Skull
- **A.** 29 bones in face, head, jaws
- **B.** 6 bones for hearing

III. Torso
- **A.** ribcage
- **B.** vertebrae
- **C.** hipbones

IV. Arms and legs
- **A.** femur and ulna
- **B.** opposable thumb
- **C.** 26 bones in foot

At Home: How can an outline help you organize your ideas for a report? Use the skeleton outline to write the first paragraph of a report about your bones.

▶ **Critical Thinking**

McGraw-Hill Language Arts Grade 4, Unit 6, Composition Skills, pages 456–457